W9-CCV-374

Adventures in an American's Literature

Norbert Blei

Adventures in an American's Literature

Norbert Blei

The Ellis Press
Peoria, Illinois

Portions of this work have appeared in *Cream City Review,* winter, 1979: "Watercolors, Indians, Black Motorcycle Jackets: Our Hero Resurrects, Self-Teaching"; and *The Madison Review,* spring, 1980: "Oh Mexico."

Published by the Ellis Press; P.O. Box 1443; Peoria, Illinois 61655. Design by David R. Pichaske. Cover poem by Norbert Blei. Typesetting by the West Bluff *Word,* Peoria. Printed by D J Graphics, Peoria and M & D Printers, Henry, Illinois.

1   2   3   4   5   6   7   8   9   10

ISBN 0-933180-41-1

for the teachers,
>Ralph Rausch
>>Ross LewAllen
>>>Jerry Bitts among them . . .

and for the students,
>Rick Meade
>>Nancy Johnson
>>>Susan O'Leary and so many others . .

I loved you everyone

Teaching is an act of love, a spiritual cohabitation, one of the few sacred relationships left in a crass secular world.

—Theodore Roethke

the author, circa 1965

Introductory Notes

This book was written in the 1960's, which may seem like many years ago to some, but which still seems like only a few days ago to me. Writers live in a different time-span.

I was not in the habit of dating manuscripts then, though it is likely that somewhere on an early draft of *Adventures In An American's Literature* I probably scratched a day, a month, and a year on the last page. I could prod my memory, rummage through cardboard boxes and files and maybe come up with the date, but it doesn't seem necessary to me anymore.

What's important is that the book is finally in print. That it is actually a first novel and that it now sees the light of day after four other books of mine have been published: *The Watercolored Word, The Hour of the Sunshine Now, Door Way,* and *The Second Novel (Becoming a Writer),* which was actually published before the first novel, though written after it.

So this is just to keep the record straight for some of my faithful readers out there, and myself as well. It's good to pause once in a while and see where the hell you are at. There isn't a whole lot of interest these days in a writer's development. Truthfully, there isn't a hell of a lot of interest in writers developing. Anyone can write a book. And has. And we all know that. The big publishing conglomerates continue to call the lucrative shots, continue to "produce" big books and big writers for big bucks. While many of the rest of us are looked upon with disdain as "regional" writers, or avant-garde writers, or literary writers, or small press people persistently plodding along the road to nowhere.

That's all right. Well, it's not all right, but that's the way it is.

So one of the things I'm saying at the moment, mainly to other struggling writers, young and old, is not to burn any manuscript you believe in, not to distrust your own imagination, not to think that the world belongs only to gothic novelists, romantic novelists, horror novelists, popular novelists, diet writers, self-help writers, etc. even though it does. Most of it anyway. But the world also belongs to those of us writers who insist on being heard. And in the long run, we just might matter more. Though I wouldn't bet on it. Because I for one won't be around to collect.

The important thing is to get the work done — to paraphrase Papa.

That's the important thing. And the next important thing is to get the work out there, one way or another, sooner or later. To find men like Morris Edelson of Quixote Press, who published *The Watercolored Word;* Rick Meade of Story Press, who published the collection of short stories, *The Hour of the Sunshine Now;* Curt Johnson of December Press, who published *The Second Novel;* and David Pichaske of The Ellis Press, who took a phenomenal financial risk to publish *Door Way* (We did it, Dave. Goddam it, we made a beautiful bestselling small press book!), and has now done this book, and will do others.

To find these kind of people, then, who believe in what you believe. And if you can't find them, then to go ahead and print the work yourself. You won't be the first. And you'll be in good company. It's important. You're important. Someone out there is waiting for, may desperately need whatever it is you have to say — if you're serious about what you say. To remember, too, that not everybody who merely *wants* to write is a writer. You've got to know that too. And you probably do. Or will discover it someday.

I just returned from New Mexico again where I came across the work of an Indian painter, Carl Beam. As a kind of parallel, he's not doing the typically commercial kind of Indian painting either. Beam is painting his own guts. He often writes on the canvas. On one of his paintings he says something like: Who is going to buy this painting? (Which is what New York is always saying about your manuscript. And not 'who'? But how many?) And Beam admits, right on the canvas, that it is not for everyone. But it is for *someone* out there. And when that person experiences it, he will know it belongs to him.

That's the way I feel about this book and all my work, whether it be poetry, short stories, novels, watercolors, books of all kinds. And so this book, too, will find its reader. It has been written especially for him or her, and it doesn't matter when. And all I'm trying to do now is suggest some kind of pattern.

And what I'm trying to suggest about that pattern is that a serious writer, writing persistently, honestly, for who knows how many years, trying all kinds of things, living all kinds of lives, in touch with all kinds of people, telling it in all manner of ways, is slowly building a body of work. *That's* important. And whether it be poetry, short stories, novels, nonfiction, whether it be published in the order in which it was written or in total disorder . . . it all comes together. It all fits. And so this book is just another part. The body of work keeps growing, taking shape.

Perhaps to glimpse some of the writer's life the past 10 years one should read his recent book of nonfiction, *Door Way*. And perhaps to understand what it took for the man to write *Door Way,* one should read his novel, *The Second Novel*. And perhaps to experience those particular moments in a writer's life, in all our lives, when clarity enters the heart as a story unfolds and changes our vision one should read a first gathering of short stories, *The Hour of the Sunshine Now*. And then, perhaps, or now, one should read *Adventures In An American's Literature* for . . . oh, call it a learning experience.

Adventures was first written in a "studio," which was actually a basement storage shed of an apartment house on the westside of Chicago. It was written during and after the author spent an appropriate time in the field of education. It was resurrected last year from under a cot in a chicken coop "studio" in Door County, Wisconsin, where I presently live and write, re-read and hardly revised at all. Not because it couldn't have been rewritten, but because I wouldn't allow myself to do so. Which goes back to the pattern I mentioned. I am a different man now, a better writer than when I first wrote the book, although always still learning the craft. And it's important to me, as a writer building a body of work, that this book reflect who and what I was at the time the book was written. What I could do then, with all that I saw and felt and thought.

It is a book that I always knew would someday be published. And that's important too. I'm just sorry it's not closer to the time I lived in its pages.

If *The Second Novel* is "about" writing, *Adventures In An American's Literature* is "about" teaching. And both books are about a lot more.

What's real is whatever you imagine.

As long as you realize what must be true.

So this one's for the teachers out there — who know themselves in their guts to be so. And for the students — who know in their own guts who the real teachers are.

May they continue to seek each other out in those ways of knowing which redeem us all.

Norbert Blei
Door County, Wisconsin
March, 1982

Adventures in an American's Literature

Part I

"A violent order is disorder"
—Wallace Stevens

Hexagram 28

Ta Kuo Excess

——————— ————
——————————————
——————————————
——————————————
——————————————
——————— ————

This hexagram symbolizes a forest submerged in a great body of
water. The Superior Man, though
standing alone, is free from fear;
he feels no discontent in with-
drawing from the world.

Early that morning in fall, before the sun rose above the lake and spread the water and the earth with light, before it entangled itself in the woods of birch, maple, and pine along the eastern edge of the far field, he walked nakedly toward the thin cedar tree some distance back behind the farmhouse, still dazed, still bleeding from the wooden skewers he had inserted through the flesh of both breasts only hours before.

With the sun almost upon him (he could see it beginning again behind his eyes, the molden arc of it rising from the dark Lake Michigan waters) he approached the tree. He tipped the bucket of rain water at hand, making a mixture of mud upon the earth's surface, and applied it to as much of his body as he could touch.

Some days before, he had procured the strongest twine that could be had from the local fishermen. He had trimmed all of the branches from the young cedar tree, and near the top of it tied the line which now hung loosely to the ground. He unraveled a portion at the end of the line, forming a 'Y,' and strengthened that juncture with a piece of monofilament, binding and tying the end.

All this he had prepared in advance.

He bent toward the earth now, picked up the two ends, and fastened them to the skewers within his flesh. Then walking north, backwards, he moved slowly till there was a tautness in the line, till, at the very moment the sun rose within range, he began to lean back, feeling his flesh pull from the hanging weight of his body, feeling the blood begin to trickle, while he looked at the sun, following its path from the rising to the setting, envisioning the final clarity and the freedom for him to begin.

He had taught himself this so far.

Days ago (or was it years?) he had begun to put down:

> It was September, another fall, and the first day of school was over. He returned to his classroom to lock up, and saw she was waiting for him in the back. Her clothes were piled high on the desk beside her. She smiled and stood up to greet him. She opened her arms, her legs. "Teach me," she whispered. He took a felt tip pen from his shirt pocket, bent and marked an 'X' above her pubic hair. He rose and passed the word, 'poem' into her mouth then dissolved between her soft thighs.

And then what? And then what? That's the way to begin a story, Hassock! Don't bore the hell out of them. Get down to basics. Get moving. Tell them how you've been trying to write this for many moons. Tell them how this is the 333rd revision of the beginning, and it still isn't true.

Tell them how you got up in the dark this morning, here in Wisconsin, went downstairs, broke an egg into the frying pan and nothing came out. 'Which came first, the chicken or the egg?' is nothing compared to the missing yolk. Where the fuck's the yolk, Hassock? There's mystery and metaphysics for you. Can you teach that? Which came first, form or content? Freedom or fantasy? Write a poem about that. Tell them a story, Hassock.

Tell them about all the women you've won with your watercolors. Tell them how they fall on the sight of your cadmium orange suns and Prussian blue moons.

Tell them about the poem you've painted on the ceiling above your head:

> The INDIAN
> wants the HUNTER WIND back
> the night pottery
> THE OPEN SECRETS OF BIRDS
> Ripened RED dances
> and
> THE SILENT RIDE
> of the
> SUN
> Nu-Mohk-Muck-a-Nah!
> (the first man)

Is that a poem, Hassock? Do you expect to get away with that kind of shit? Is that what you teach? Who are you, the New Indian or something just because you walk around the woods bareass all the time and call yourself Tawa? How many names do you have?

Begin somewhere, will you? What the hell's the story?

Tell them about the hand that erases.

TELL THEM ABOUT THE FIRE IN YOUR HEAD.

Tell them how you flunked catechism in the third grade because you could never memorize the answer to: Who is God?

Tell them how you got hung up in teaching.

Tell them how you always wanted to become a priest.

Tell them how you spent a summer's day trying to watch a sunflower move.

4

Tell them about the Sun Dance, the Sioux, Looking at the Sun.
Say something, Hassock, Tawa, Blazen . . . whoever you are.
Tell them how in the darkness and light of thunderstorms, you push the small boat into the water and await a connection.
Tell them how you try to paint the moon in the dark.
Tell them how you flunked religion in the third grade because the Mystical Body of Christ was beyond you.
Tell them how you get so lonesome in Wisconsin at night that you take out that letter from Green-eyes and cry.

> . . . please accept this gift as one of the few things I can give you in thanks for all you've given me — an introduction to poetry and Henry Miller, the experience of Mexico, an appreciation of some (to me) new art and philosophy, and most importantly, an assist with a giant butterfly net to help me re-capture my free spirit.
>
> Love,
> Green-eyes

Tell them about the mosquito bites on your ass, Tawa.
Were the Indians ever plagued by mosquito bites? Have you found that yet in your studies of the Native American?
Isn't Far East and Far West the same? Or are you getting too far ahead in your story?
Tell them how you dance the polka alone with all the old music still inside your head.
Come on, Hassock. Come on, Blazen. Come on, Tawa, dance! . . . Nu-mohk-muck-a-nah!

Sitting down . . . writing this . . . beginning before other things begin to happen. Is this how I sound? After the silence? I am in Door County, Wisconsin. Living every day and night as it comes. Getting acquainted with weather. Getting acquainted with nature. Making poems, painting watercolors. Still. Human contact? Little. Yesterday, the girl from the local store stopped by with food. My little Katchina doll. We walked through the fields behind the house. We made love in the tall weeds, insects buzzing around our sweaty bodies. I never spoke, but through my hands.

This is how I see my life now. Back home in Chicago, I lived and worked in a basement. I wrote a story about that once, if I remember. I am always telling stories about myself. It can't be helped.

Once I had plans. Even for this. Elaborate plans as to precisely how I would construct this story. I forget... I've forgotten. At the moment, I see myself looking at all the watercolors surrounding me in this room. I feel alive about them and can't really believe they're all mine. They are not all very good, but they are still mine. And they delight me. 'Flowers, Trees, Sky and Sun' . . . childish. Children . . . how do they do it? Don't think.

Tone. A writer's tone. How do I sound? Is the silence of the written word still silence? Tone . . . who and what you are?

Tone can be dishonest. People will believe you. But never know you — like Henry James, who is not an adventure in American literature at all. Saroyan is an adventure. You can't mistake him for anyone else. Sometimes in class, when I really felt dismayed, when perhaps Hester's Scarlet 'A' became too much of a punishment for all of us, I would turn to Saroyan for life. Miller, too. The only writers worth reading are those who lived adventures and are dying to tell about them. Spirits who may certainly affect your own. We should all bring about changes in each other.

I wrote Saroyan once, exalting in his madness. He never answered. He didn't have to. I wrote to Henry Miller once too. He answered and thanked me for my watercolor.

I began with watercolors because of him, because of what he said in TO PAINT IS TO LOVE AGAIN and "The Angel Is My Watermark." Looking at his watercolors, swept up by his tone, his sense of life and self. It is better by far to be the artist. To be the creative act. Miller has the magic of making us so.

Sometimes I write on my watercolors like Patchen. Kenneth Patchen. Jesus, another adventure in American literature.

I write on paintings to be heard as well as seen. Take this painting I just finished. A painting of the countryside around me. The colors are indescribable. They are masses of greens and blues and reds and oranges that flow and finally dry into strange forms that invariably speak of me.

I work around the dry forms then with a pen and mark them: Open Fields, Road, Lake, Woods, Pasture with Cows, Wildflowers, Cherry Trees, Sky, and Sun. I continue filling in the white spaces with words. Sometimes words that don't mean a damn thing. Sometimes a story, a poem, or a quotation, like the one from Meister Eckhart: "Only the hand that erases can write the true thing."

Sometimes only one word like "Menominee." Say it softly to yourself, Men...om...in...ee. Or, "Nu-mohk-muck-a-nah!" Put words on watercolors, and you'll experience them new everytime. That's the way of watercolors — change.

When I discover myself in a really good one, a watercolor I may want to keep forever, I wrap it up and mail it to someone. I never keep a watercolor I truly love. Like this one I've just finished. I think I'll send it to Princess K., a student of mine sometime ago that I can't forget. She's probably in most of the watercolors I've painted in Wisconsin so far. She and Green-eyes. This one for Princess K. because she loved the earth and imagined her survival.

But I won't send it to her yet. I will watch it get better with time. Watercolors do that. Sometimes I live with them a long time before I understand all they have to tell me. And only *then* is it time to give them away, forget them, surprise myself with new ones or these others that keep appearing on my walls.

What keeps bringing me back to this one here, the one I did before the thunderstorm the other night, is what it has to say. I'm not sure I like the colors very much yet. The words pull harder, and I'm now just beginning to hear them:

> When you paint,
> you should make
> mistakes.
>
>   Sometimes you make many mistakes.
>
> If you make a lot of
> good mistakes,
> you make a Great Painting.

This is not
     a
       Great Painting
because of this very bad mistake.

                          But overall it is not
                          a totally bad painting.

     And when you paint,
         whatever you do,
             you should make mistakes
     good
     and
     bad.

What I'm really trying to do here is move away from art. This happens to be an idea I just rediscovered in one of my notebooks. It must be recent, though. It's a Wisconsin idea, not one that appeared to me back in Chicago. Chicago doesn't speak to me that way. To get away from art, from anything, is to find it. Which sounds like Zen. But I don't know anything about Zen either. Not yet.

I was talking about beginning this story I'm trying to tell. Actually, I've finished it already, if you know what I mean. But I want to go back to one of the beginnings.

But first I'm going to go downstairs, take a shot of brandy and some coffee, then go out and look at the sun for awhile. It's difficult for me to remain inside on days like this.

Back home in Chicago, though, down in the basement I would never know what the day held. It was always a surprise walking up and into it: rain, snow, wind, sun, cloudiness.

Hassock, tell them about the canoe you made of birch bark. How you painted the sun on the front and the moon on the back. How you pushed off with it into the lake. How the fucker sunk and you almost drowned. Some Indian, Tawa!

As I've said many times before, once I had plans. The last time I tried to tell this story I had all kinds of outlines, notes, journal entries. And symbols. I was always very big on symbols. That's how I was taught to believe in things that had no answers in Catholic grammar school. That's the way I was taught to appreciate literature in college. So when I began to create, symbols came from everywhere.

So back when I had plans, when I was very conscious of form and art, the book was supposed to begin like this:

There are only beginnings, and crime is as good a depth
to begin as any.

Very classy opening. Designed to lead the reader deeper and deeper into the story till the very end, which reflects all the truth and beauty of the beginning.

We'll get back to our story in a moment, as they say. But first . . . I'm concerned with beginnings and endings, how there are so many of them, and how, in the end, they are all the same. Titles also interest me. Any one book could be called almost anything.

I once thought the title of this book was IN THE SHADOW OF THE TEMPLE, which came from Gibran's THE PROPHET, a gift from one of my students some time ago. I've gone beyond that now, but what I liked then was the word "shadow," a true enough symbol for the dark side of my subject.

8

Then I thought I would call the book STAND OUT OF MY LIGHT, something Alexander the Great's teacher told him at the proper time.

Teacher. That's what this is all about: teaching.

To get back to our story:

> There are only beginnings and crime is as good a beginning as any.

Which still holds true. There is a very thin line between the criminal and the creative.

Hassock, get on with the story for Christ's sake.

I am in high school in a Slavic neighborhood on the westside of Chicago. I am dressed in the soft armor which is necessary for my existence — black leather. I wear a beautiful motorcycle jacket with a studded silver cross on my back. Shiny metal zippers at the wrist that press the leather to the forearm like another layer of skin. Zipper-slashed pockets all over the front, and even one behind me at the small of the back. And a thick heavy zipper with a rabbit's foot pull to run up and down the front of the jacket.

At the very bottom, around the waist, a belt like licorice with a silver buckle to cup in my hand, pulling tighter and tighter, cinching everything in strength. Snap buttons of silver on the lapels to pop with attention as I stand in the midst of others and slowly begin the ritual of loosening the jacket, releasing the pressure of the burgeoning life inside. The leather breathes.

Hard, high-heeled engineer boots. Buckles at top and bottom. Silver studded nails which I hammer around the heels. Heavy cleats which announce my arrival and departure down the marble halls of the high school, the concrete walks of the neighborhood, the asphalt of the streets.

This is the 1950's in America.

My hair is long, black, slick with hair cream, swept back into solid waves of the D.A., the duck-ass style. I carry a rat-tailed comb in my back pocket, forever running it through my hair till my wrist grows limp.

My sideburns are long and curly.

I wear faded blue Levis, tight across the ass and crotch, the balls bulging through, ready to grab at any time in answer to any smart-ass remark: "Here, buddy, here's yours. I got you by the head!"

A wide western belt with a heavy buckle of hammered silver and copper birds.

There is even more to me than this:

A black cap with white braid; black leather gloves; and a white silk scarf stolen from the old man's dresser. And mirrored, military sun glasses lifted from the local drugstore.

I walk straight.

I walk tall.

I make footsteps that are hard to forget.

I carry everything, especially myself.

I smirk in the secrecy of my pockets — zippered-tight mouths of tiny teeth, little chains dangling, concealing everything I need to live for the time being. From marijuana to holy pictures; from condoms to skeleton keys; from rosaries to brass knuckles; from loose change to a 6 inch blade that springs to life at a thumb's touch; from a Sacred Heart medal to yellow pencil stubs gnawed down to the lead.

I carry it all on my person, everywhere I wish to go or find myself; home, neighborhood, church, classroom. The classroom, especially has need of the armor and dress that is unmistakably me.

The hero, you see, is a difficult role to feign. The "motorcycle kid" in the absence of the Big Bike, is a gangster without a gun, a cowboy without a horse. He needs the hardware for personification and performance. And in the end, he needs someone to spread his word around, though his finest acts may be illuminated by solitariness and silence, and lead to nothing.

Listen.

One day you find yourself in high school, and you're there because society says that's where you belong for your age. And that's where they keep you till you're old enough to quit, till you're kicked out, till you graduate.

I never liked the whole scene. Maybe I felt I wasn't smart enough. Maybe I was just bored. Maybe I felt too old for homework and school activities. I was doing almost everything grownups were doing and still I had to go to school when all I really wanted to do was have a job, buy a car, and screw around with the gang. An average neighborhood teenager, often finding himself in trouble.

High school is a challenge all right. Everything about the place — the dungeon basement where I take shop courses in woodworking and auto mechanics, the frosted windows everywhere, the ugly fly-shitted light bulbs coming down on you, hanging there by dusty chains — everything's designed to hold you in place to make you forget there's an outside and maybe the sun is shining, the beautiful women are walking the streets downtown, the forest preserves are green and quiet, the White Sox are playing at Comiskey Park. Even the classroom clocks keep making jerking noises every minute to remind you where you're at.

Teachers question your every move. Librarians frisk you at the door. There are guards — student government finks — in all the halls, all the time, including the cafeteria. Every goddam entrance to the school is guarded so you can't step out to sneak a quick smoke.

I'm pissed as soon as I step into the building. "Get a haircut," a teacher I don't even know yells at me. "Don't bang your locker like that," some pimp of a hall guard warns me. "Don't ever sit at this table again for lunch." "What are you doing in the halls at this time of day?" "Why aren't you in class now, young man?" "Take off that jacket and leave it in your locker."

"No, you can't go to the washroom now," Maaze, the civics teacher tells me.

"Why?"

"Listen, smart guy, you're in class now. Go back to your desk."

"We're supposed to be reading. I forgot my book in the locker. All I want to do is go to the john and pick up my book on the way back. Is that a real threat? Just give me a pass, huh Maaze?"

"Sit down. Take off that jacket. And get your hands out of your pockets, you cold or something?"

"Listen, Maaze, I've got to take a piss." And then I whip out a big rubber finger from one of my pockets and start jabbing it in front of his face.

How to be popular in one easy lesson. Instant gratification. The class is with me. It's *my* class now. Some of the guys stand up and cheer. The broads are giggling and clapping. When Maaze pulls me out of the classroom, digging hard with his fingers into the leather sleeves of my jacket, thinking he's hurting me, but he's not, I give out the old cycle yell, "ZOOM! ZOOM!," flicking my cupped hands like I'm bearing down real hard, ready to dig out.

They take away my rubber finger at the Dean's Office and try to make me empty my other pockets. I won't. For all this I get a two day suspension when all I wanted to do was take a piss and get my book.

My classes are all dummy classes except for one. In the dummy classes it's taken for granted you're lazy and stupid and will never be able to cut it in college.

I've got this counselor, Wrankel, a real ass, who gives me all these tests

11

and then tells me how bad I scored, showing me on some graphs just how bad I am compared to everybody else in the country, everything but reading, that is, and how I'll never get into college, and I should be thinking in terms of terminal education. A mechanic, a barber, something I'd enjoy doing with my hands.

Fuck you, I say to him under my breath. Right now I'd enjoy putting my fist into your puss. It's like he's got my whole life planned on that sheet of paper. And I don't mind so much he thinks I might make a good mechanic, what I really mind about this shithead is his smile, his being so fucking sure of me that I'm nothing.

So he says the tests show I'm going nowhere, and it's nowhere they put me: the dummy classes where they just sit with you. Nobody teaches you nothing. Maybe once in a while they read to you like that old fart, Miss Nickelson, who asks you questions from the back of the book where most of the answers are written out anyway by the dummy who had her and the same book last year.

Maaze doesn't even do that. Maaze gets you in class, takes roll like it's the most important thing he's ever done in his life, then tells you to just sit still and be quiet while he reads the newspaper the whole hour.

Maaze is a prick. I write that in his book. And draw a picture of him like that —with ears. I dig my knife into the top of the desk, carving out his face. "Maaze Sucks," I scrape in there deeper and deeper with a pen.

You screw off as much as you can without getting caught. You play it always, everything, as close as you can for excitement. You get caught — you lose. If you got some broads around you, it's even better. It gives it a little more of an edge.

You pass them dirty notes, anything to make them laugh. You can pull all kinds of shit with them in the dummy classes as long as you're quiet. You can even feel some of them up the way Kretchel does in science where you got partners, two to a table. Kretchel going to town there right in front of old man Borden, playing around with his Bunsen burner that isn't working again because the boys have screwed it up. Kretchel's got a whole hand into her pants, and I'm getting hornier than hell just glancing behind occasionally, watching her legs begin to vibrate under that table.

"Cut it out, Kretchel!" I yell. "I can't take it. I'm willing my hot rocks to science !"

"You, back there in the black jacket," says Borden.

"Yes?"

"Go to the Dean's Office. Tell them I'm transferring you to a study hall. I don't need the likes of you in my class."

Study halls. The last corral. I already have three. And nothing to study.

I never had a teacher who was worth a shit except for an English teacher who was a fag and a history teacher who was a Jew — both rare birds in my neighborhood. Catholic grammar school was a complete blowout with all those penguin nuns pecking away at you. The priests, most of them were all right and seemed to know the score, but they were never around much.

But this fag teacher, Castrati, is really something. I wonder how they let a guy like this teach. He reads poetry to us with this fairy voice from a book only a few of us have, called ADVENTURES IN AMERICAN LITERATURE.

We tease the hell out of him, but it never seems to bug him. He never tells us to be quiet. And it's only in his class that I talk about thing's I'd never talk about anywhere else. Stuff not even in the textbook. Things about dying and being in love and being a free man.

He's always reading from some guy named Whitman who was a fucking male nurse or something. "Did he wear a white dress, and white stockings, and a white cape?" I asked.

We run all over him. We're always out of hand. "Hey, I got your Walty right here," one of the guys yells right to Castrati's face. But he never gets mad. Never sends anyone to the Dean's.

A few of the guys met him in the washroom once. He was standing there, combing his hair in a big wave up front, smiling, prettying himself up as usual. Nodding and winking to all the guys who knew him.

"Hey, Castrati, how they hanging?" yells Kretchel, who is sitting on the pot, watching him through the reflection in the mirror. "I got something for you."

"You think you're man enough," smiles Castrati.

"A man 7 inches tall is enough for you," answers Kretchel, everybody laughing, even Castrati. I laughed too. But I felt depressed, sorry for him.

"Knock it off, Kretchel," I said.

"How about a blowjob, Castrati?" another guy yells.

"Hey, Castrati, I got a mouthful for you," someone else yells.

The place was filled with laughter, filled with guys yelling all kinds of dirty stuff, most of the guys who didn't even know Castrati, never even had him for a teacher. Even a lot of the goody-two-shoes, the smart-asses who got all the good teachers. Some of those fuckers were worse than us.

And Castrati just stands there, taking it all. No protection. No threats.

What's worse, the jerk is even smiling. He should grab some of those wise bastards and punch 'em in the mouth.

"Fuck off, you guys. Fuck off!" I zip up my jacket, kick open the door, and leave. I can't take that kind of shit.

Moss was the Jew teacher, the other one I liked. I don't know how I got into Moss' class. It had to be a mistake. My great counselor, Wrankel, must have fucked up; his bell curve must have wound up in his asshole because they saved guys like Moss for the sharp kids, not the dummies like me.

So there I am sitting around in a room full of daisies. None of my people around. All my people knew was that Moss was a Jew. "You got Moss? The Jew?"

"Yeah, Moss."

"He's a Jew."

"So what? What the fuck's that supposed to mean? You're a Bohunk."

"Yeah, but he's a kike."

Moss was thin and bald and wore steel-rimmed glasses. He never got up from his desk. Never once did I see him get on his feet in that classroom. When he had to use the blackboard, he'd just lean over backwards in the chair and write sitting down. I used to wonder if he had any legs at all.

Sometimes he'd call you to the front of the desk to discuss your paper.

He was the only teacher I ever did any homework for. He liked what you did even if you were all wrong. He'd always say: "There's a good idea in there. Read some other books. See what they have to say about the same thing."

He was always throwing different names at us. Different books. We never used the textbook except to look at maps. All we ever learned from Moss was that everybody saw history a little different. And nobody really agreed about anything.

Moss, I guess, was a real teacher. You never watched the clock in his class. The time always went by fast. He ripped through chapter after chapter of European history from all kinds of books, but mostly from his own head. I could see everything the way he talked about it. And he took beautiful swipes at things I never heard anyone bitch about before. It wasn't American history, but he kept bringing America into it. Once he told us how he took a Negro professor friend of his into the teacher's cafeteria, and everybody just about shit. "God bless America," he'd say. And then smile.

14

The Spanish Civil War was one of his favorite topics. Our foreign policy and power politics would really piss him off. "Dulles," he said, "First shook his finger, then shook his fist . . . then shook all over."

"The world is just a huge firecracker," he'd say. "And some idiot is always running around with a lighted match."

I came out of his class with all kinds of things to talk about but no one to talk to. I never mixed with the other kids in class. My motorcycle jacket alone was enough for them. I stuck to myself and read a lot of the books Moss would talk about. Once in a while I'd say something in class. Most of the time I'd listen and lap it all up. I'd run into one of the guys in the halls after class and say: "Hey, you know what Moss said today?"

"The Jew?"

"He said Lincoln was a big phony. Not exactly, of course, but he wasn't really anti-slavery. Neither was Jefferson, you know."

"So what?"

"Well, he's great, this guy! He's always coming up with stuff like this. A lot of the stuff they crammed down our throats in grammar school was just a bunch of bullshit. The Popes . . . you know what about the Popes? They had all kinds of broads on the side. Did you know that? Mistresses. Sister Mary Anna never told us that! Poontang, man. The Pope! Can you imagine? And you know what else? We're nothin but a bunch of goddam thieves and murderers. We stole this whole fucking country from the Indians. And we killed them, man. Tons and tons of them. Fucking dead Indians everywhere, just to get the land."

"Who gives a shit. He's a fucking Hebe, ain't he? And I heard he's a Commie."

The guys just didn't give a shit about Moss no matter what I told them. They'd never have him for a teacher. They were all in the dummy classes doing current events quizzes, copying everybody's answers, correcting them once in a while when the teacher felt like reading the answers.

And even when I got home, no one would listen. The old man and the old lady were foreigners. They could hardly speak English. The old man could, when he wanted to. All they knew was work, fixing things up around the bungalow, and saving money. The old man, always hanging his ass on some ladder crawling up to fix the gutters or the roof. The old lady always bent over in her goddam backyard garden. I was supposed to go to school and get the education they were never able to get. Same old shit. Washington was a dollar bill. Lincoln was a penny. That was American history to them. Though the name Hoover brought on curses. And Franklin Delano Roosevelt was some kind of a god.

15

School was the proving ground. Between classes, during study halls, lunch, gym, we go over the day's adventures, planning new ones for after school or the next day. We are interested in only one thing: destruction. The guy, any one of us, who can really fuck up the works. Cutting up books in the library, stealing a few, fighting in the halls, tearing the shithouse apart, smarting off to teachers — getting them pissed off enough to fight. Sometimes we would work together, but it's always better alone. Then everyone has to listen to how you did it. You alone.

Inside school, the most you can do, the only way they'll remember your name, is to destroy things. Fights, cheating, stealing, back-talk, all come after breaking desks, windows, lockers. Pulling shades ... wham! right off the fucking rollers. "Sorry, teach. I guess I missed the catch." Anything like this, even filling a teacher's desk with Kotex, will tell the world who you are. And it's even better outside, after school. Especially at night.

On the outside you can start right in the teacher's parking lot, filling gas tanks with sand, stealing hub caps, filling them with stones, or just denting them with your foot. Slashing tires. Breaking hood ornaments. Once I took a hammer and puckered up the whole top of Maaze's car. BAM! BAM! BAM!

But the real time, the big time, is night. You and nobody else. Sooner or later you drift into the real thing. Sooner or later you're really up against it with the cops. And it's none of this candyshit of being taken to school in a squad car because you were caught ditching. It's more like the squad car pulling up to the school and yanking you right out of the goddam class in front of everybody. You don't forget that.

I had all the credentials for crime. For years I had been growing up to it. A few things probably held me back. The church for a while. The old man and the old lady a little. But now with the jacket, with high school and the guys and the broads, now was the time to begin.

Oh, I had worked at it a little before with friends of mine from the neighborhood. Stealing cars for the hell of it. Taking the babes for joyrides. "Hey, baby, you put out? Hop in." There's nothing to stealing cars.

Shoplifting we did almost everyday after school. Almost anything a guy could need could be lifted from dime stores, hardware stores, drugstores and groceries.

One of the coolest jobs I ever pulled was lifting the motorcycle jacket. It was a big department store downtown, Chicago, where all the stuff was hanging out on open racks. I walked in with a navy blue jacket, walked around a rack of workshirts a couple of times. My whole body began shaking. I quick pulled the navy jacket off, threw it under the rack of workshirts, and slipped on the motorcycle jacket from the rack on the other side.

Nothing to it. I walked up and down the aisle a little more to calm down, then went right up to a salesman with the new jacket hanging open on me like I was warm, and asked him where the work boots were. He pointed to another part of the floor, and I thanked him and walked away.

Next day in school I told my girl, Rita, about it, and she couldn't believe how I did it so easy and pretty soon it was all over school, and I walked down those halls like a goddam parade.

And that night, for the first time, Rita really put out for me. I got plenty from broads before, even in grammar school, but mainly it was feeling a little titty on Saturday afternoons at the Town show.

Rita was a tough little Polack and would never let me go too far. I could get her bra off, and her pants maybe halfway down, but that was all. She'd really piss me off. I could hardly hold it in my pants and she'd keep saying, "No, no. I can't. We can't do it. Not yet. Not now."

I knew she put out more for other guys before, and that's what really pissed me off. "Goddam it. What about all the other guys that got in to you? Why them and not me?"

"It's different with you."

"What's different? I'm gonna burst! I'm going blind!"

"You're different, that's all. The other guys just grab and don't say nothing. You talk to me and make me feel good. You really like me, and I like you, you know?"

"Yeah, yeah, I know. So I'm left here with a case of blue balls."

But she was right. I really did like her. I liked to hold her, I liked to kiss her, I just liked to be with her, to give her presents, like my old Indian head ring, take her to movies, buy her smokes and hamburgers and strawberry malts.

I think I loved her. When she would grab me by the balls once in a while, I think I even wanted to marry her. I wanted to marry her right away because she was sexy and could make me laugh and could make me feel good by bragging about me to everybody else.

That night I told her about the motorcycle jacket, and she told everybody else. I had a hardon all the while I walked to her house, just thinking about her. She was short, with brown hair and gray eyes and a beautiful round set of tits that I loved to squeeze. And tonight I was gonna get hold of them again and spread those legs and work on that silky box of hers.

I was wearing my new jacket, engineer boots, and a white silk scarf. Going up the wooden steps of her front porch, I punched my heels down hard to let her know who it was.

We walked over to the park for a while. Smoked, talked, held hands and waited for the streetlights to go on. As it got dark, we walked down the alley to her house, my hand in her blouse all the way, and hid in the garage.

The place stunk from oil and gas. I couldn't see a thing at first. She led me to an old sofa covered with newspapers. There was a window above it with a little bit of light coming in from thet back porch of the next door neighbor. I threw all the junk off the sofa, and we started French kissing.

"Let me take your jacket off," she said.

"I can take it off myself."

"No, let me."

She started on all the zippers and then the snap buttons — pop! pop! pop! "This is fun," she said. She unloosened the belt and pulled down slowly on the front zipper. She ran her hands inside my jacket then began rubbing my crotch. I ached. What a broad!

I began undressing her while she helped with the bra and then bent down and began working me over some more.

"Do you have any rubbers?" she said.

"In the back of the jacket. I got them at the gas station." Her fingers went behind me, searching for the jacket.

"Here, let me fix it," she said.

She lay back, her head on the arm rest, and pulled me into her like a dumb dog or something. She dug into my waist with her nails and kept everything going.

"Slower, slow down," she said and began to moan.

But I couldn't slow down. I kept going like hell till it was all over, and I loved her more than anything in my life. I was ready to marry her — quit school, find a job, settle down.

We played around with each other for a while and screwed again. I was beginning to get dizzy from the smell of gas. I heard a door bang, and I was afraid someone was coming. A dog began barking and then a woman began hollering for her kids to come home.

"Don't worry," Rita said. "Nobody's going to come in here."

I got into her once more, but it was all over. I was too beat to do anything. I just knelt over her and kissed her nipples over and over again.

The next night I began robbing houses and small stores. I carried all kinds of tools in my jacket: pliers, a screwdriver, a glass cutter, a small flashlight and skeleton keys.

Houses were the easiest to get into. I'd keep a watch on them from the alleys, waiting for the people to leave. Saturday nights were the best. Even if the people left a light on to throw you, I'd always ring the back doorbell first and listen if someone was coming. The slightest sound and I'd take off like hell down the gangway.

A couple of times I got caught standing at the door, but it was easy enough to talk my way out of it by making up a name and asking if the person lived there. Most people sympathize with you when you have the wrong house. Sometimes they even go for the phone book to help you out.

But when no one answers, and a dog isn't barking, then I move fast. Always the back door. Skeleton keys work nine times out of ten. And when they don't, there's always a basement window that's unlocked or can be pried open.

Once I'm inside, I'm on fire. My head starts bubbling. I can't even describe how it feels. If you ever tried to steal anything, the first time you ever tried, that's a little bit like how it feels. Scared. Excited.

For one thing, you're never really sure there's no one else in the house. The people could be sleeping. Or sometimes a dog won't make a sound until you just about step on him. Then either you tame him petting him, feeding him something, or else choke the sonofabitch.

Always hit the bedrooms first, that's what the guys tell you. The bedroom is the bank. Usually there isn't enough time to tear the whole house apart anyway. The dressers, maybe some of the closets. But if there's nothing there, clear out. Any bedroom should give you at least 10 bucks. And if you feel cool, if everything's quiet, you can scrouge around carefully and with luck maybe end up with a bankroll of $100 or more.

Once you're in the place more than fifteen minutes, you begin to loosen up. The place becomes more like home. You begin to recognize chairs and tables and lamps. You begin to feel like you know the people.

The kitchen. I always like the kitchen. Sometimes I sit down at the table and eat in the dark. I think about the people who live there, what they look like, what the old man does for a living. Sometimes I feel like leaving them a letter, "Hey, it's me, your friendly thief. Just stopped by tonight to say hello. The cake was good and so was the cold chicken. Nice looking daughter you got. Saw her picture on the dresser. Thanks for everything."

When I tell the guys at school about this, what a great thing it would be to do sometime, they just tell me I'm nuts. "How do you think of stuff like that?" they say. Shit, I just feel like that. I can't help it. I think some of the stuff they do is nuts.

All they think about is wrecking a place if they don't find enough dough. I think that's nuts. I'm glad to find just a few bucks stashed away, something to eat, maybe a beer, and then clear out. That's good enough for me.

But when they don't find any money, they rip the fucking sofas, break the furniture, smear food all over the kitchen. One guy I know, Makraw, even took a crap on the cocktail table once.

My problem is I can never let another guy get one up on me. Anybody dares me — roll drunks, rob stores, steal purses, beat somebody up — I do it.

I've got a pair of blue suede box-toe loafers I wear once in a while to school for dressing up times. Electric blue pegged pants, stitched seams, button-down flap pockets on the back. A pink-on-pink shirt with a Billy Eckstine collar, black onyx cufflinks, and a Windsor knot on my white tie. Cool. Rock and roll time, Bill Hailey and the Comets.

One time during gym, a kid swiped my blue suede box-toe loafers. I had to wear gym shoes the rest of the day. About a week later one of the guys got the bead on the character who swiped my shoes — Joe Kriz. A wiseass. Upper classman. Very cool with all the babes. Hot shot on the dance floor.

"You'll never get those shoes back," they egged me on. "Chicken shit."

I waited for the Friday night teen dance at St. Paul's. I waited till everybody was out on the floor dancing, and then they all pulled back and made a circle around Kriz and some broad he picked up from another school. I opened my jacket, then unzipped the side pockets feeling for the knucks. I just stood there in that circle, looking at those shoes Kriz was dancing in. No doubt about it. Those were my fucking shoes.

I waited till he was dancing with his back towards me, then slowly walked out on the dance floor, tapped him on the shoulder with my left hand, and when he turned around, pulled my right hand with the knucks from my pocket and buried it into his gut. He doubled over, starting puking and coughing, and while he was curled upon the floor, I took the shoes off and put them in the pockets of my motorcycle jacket.

I was scared shitless. I could hardly talk. Only a couple of times early in grammar school did I ever get into any fights, and most of those was pushing and shoving and choking and pulling hair with maybe a star punch here and there.

As soon as I hit Kriz, I felt sorry for him. I felt strong, I felt top dog, I felt I could kill . . . but I felt weak as well. Weak and scared. I didn't like myself. Yet out of nowhere I hear myself standing over him and saying: "Don't you ever fucking take anything from me again!" And then I started to walk away, but then I turned back, bent down, rolled him over on his back, undid his belt, and right in front of everybody, I pantsed him. I left him there in his white BVD's walked back into the circle, felt hands slapping me on the back, and then ran to Rita's house, laughing and crying and scared down the streets.

"You know," my buddy, Tazlio, said to me one time. "I know a guy who wants to rob a church."

"Bullshit. What the hell's in a church? The poor-box?"

"No, I'm not shittin' you. This guy has it all set up. He's after gold. And silver. And it's perfect. The place is open all the time. Let's try it."

"Where do you get this gold shit? You mean the altar? You mean the candlesticks? The tabernacle? . . . Sure, the tabernacle with the chalices and everything. Yeah, sure, that's it. But what the fuck . . . I mean robbing a goddam church! That's crazy! Hey, can you see Father Kiley saying mass on Sunday, and he goes up the steps to the altar and holy Christ, the tabernacle's gone! Sorry, Kiley, no boozing today. The wine has disappeared! A miracle!"

"Yeah! Yeah!"

"Man, wouldn't that be something? Those chalices must be worth some good dough. Where do we dump them? Down in Jewtown, huh? Down on Maxwell Street early Sunday morning. Where else? 'Hey, buddy, wanna buy a hot chalice? Or how about a hot tabernacle for the top of the TV?'"

I walked into St. Paul's late one Saturday night. Confessions were just about over. Only a few lights were on under the Stations of the Cross. Mostly the candles were flickering in the red vigil lights. Jesus, Mary and Joseph, the Sacred Heart, the Infant of Prague, the whole crew, all of them seemed to move in the shadows as the candlelight ran back and forth over their faces and robes. The church was always very mysterious to me. Very spooky.

The only priest still hearing confessions was Father Kiley. You could always hear him all over the church, he was so damn loud. "AND WHEN WAS YOUR LAST CONFESSION? SAY TEN OUR FATHERS AND TEN HAIL MARYS AND PRAY THAT THE BLESSED VIRGIN WILL GUIDE YOU." The bastard probably did it on purpose just to embarrass the person. I know Kiley. He pulled all kinds of shit.

You weren't supposed to listen to the priests or the people in the confessionals if they were too loud, but I could never keep my mind on anything else. I was always listening for some beautiful broad in there confessing all her great sins to the priest, mainly how she's been fucking everything in sight. I wanted to hear what the priest would say. How he'd handle something like that. And I was anxious to see her face again when she came out. And then what I really wanted was for her to fuck me.

Whoever was in there now was sure catching it from Kiley "TWENTY-FIVE OUR FATHERS AND TWENTY-FIVE HAIL MARY'S," for penance. Christ, somebody must have killed somebody.

I was kneeling down about ten pews in front of the confessional so even when the guy walked out I couldn't see him so good. He walked straight to the altar railing and began saying his penance.

No one else was in the church now but me and Kiley. I heard the confessional door click open. Kiley stepped out.

"Are you here for confession?"

"No, Father," I answered kind of softly without looking back at him.

"Well then, that's it," he said to himself. I heard him switch off the confessional light, genuflect at the holy water fountain in the back of the church, then push the door open and leave.

No one else came in.

It was close to 10 o'clock, and the guy was still up there saying penance. Finally a noise echoed throughout the church, and I saw him stand up, genuflect, and come down the aisle toward me.

I kept my head bowed low, my lips moving in silent prayer, rattling off every prayer I could remember from grammar school. The back door opened and swayed shut. I was alone.

I began unzipping the front of my jacket, the sleeves, the slash pockets. I waited a few more minutes and then slowly got up from the pew and walked all the way down the center aisle to the altar, trying hard to keep my boots from clicking.

I started to smile. I started thinking crazy things again. I started saying out loud, "Here I come, God, ready or not. Drop your red heart! Hey, St. Joe, what do you know?"

I was like a priest at the head of some procession. The Feast of the Virgin Mary or something. All I needed was a silver crucifix on top of a long pole and kids and grownups following behind me.

The jacket swung loose on me. My cap stuck out of the back pocket of my Levis. I unknotted the white silk scarf till it hung down, the fringes almost touching my knees like a surplice.

It wasn't too dark at the altar. There was enough candlelight. Above me, all around me, the stained glass windows that I used to stare at till I went into a trance at Sunday mass — the blood reds and purples, the yellows and oranges like solid hunks of fire — all the colors seemed burn-

22

ed out, dead. Sometimes during mass I thought I was going crazy watching all that color. I wanted to scream. Sometimes one statue would catch my eye, looking right at me, and I'd watch it for the whole hour while it stared, smiled, and seemed to move from side to side.

I pushed this all in the back of my mind. I tried to think, instead, of Rita. I thought of unhooking her bra, and then holding my head to her nipples.

Then everything in the church was the way it always was, although things really were not the same. The floor squeaked. I thought I saw the arm of a statue move. I started to think of Rita again, listening for her moan.

When I got to the altar railing, with the statue of the Sacred Heart guarding one side, his hand in the air like a cop holding up traffic, the big red apple of a heart sticking out of him . . . and the Blessed Virgin Mary waiting on the other side, standing on a snake in her bare feet, I feel for the latch on the center gate and swing it wide open the way the altar boys do for weddings and special masses.

The altar steps are soft, thickly carpeted — the same steps where I once practiced after school to become an altar boy. I kneel down, make the sign of the cross . . . and begin to say mass, playing both priest and altar boy.

"In Nomine Patris, et Filii, et Spiritus Sancti. Amen."

The Latin, the movements of a priest and altar boy . . . none of this has ever left me.

"Introibo ad altare Dei," (I will go unto the altar of God.)

"Ad Deum qui laetificat juventutum meam," (To God, the joy of my youth.)

I genuflect, gathering an invisible black cassock from entangling my heels, and move toward the bells for the Sanctus. I pick them up and sharply ring them three times:

"Sanctus, Sanctus, Sanctus, Dominus Deus, Sabaoth. Plani sunt caeli et terra gloria tua. Hosana in excelsis. Benedictus qui venit in nomine Domini. Hosana in excelsis."

Stepping up to the altar, I recall how big the damn thing is. I feel like a little kid reaching up to a banquet table. The crucifix seems 30 feet high. There He hangs, the King of Kings, looking down at me with that sad face, that bloody head and crown of thorns.

"How's it going, man? Does it hurt when they pound nails in your hands and feet? I ought to climb up there sometime and get you dressed for Sunday mass —jacket, cap, boots, gloves . . . the whole works."

There are two candles burning on each side of the altar and the tabernacle in the center like a golden bucket with a funnel on top. The Wizard of Oz comes to mind. The Tin Man.

So many times I've seen the priest open the tabernacle door to take out the wine and bread. So many times I've wondered what was really inside there. In school the nuns would tell us Christ lived in there. And when I was just a little kid, I used to think that inside the tabernacle it was like a house, with a kitchen, a front room, a bedroom, even a toilet.

I stand up on my toes now and reach way over to grab the doors. I dig my fingernails deep around the edges till they hurt. Is the damn thing locked, or are there such heavy springs holding it that I don't have enough leverage to pull them open?

I reach into the back pocket of my jacket for the small screwdriver and begin prying the doors open. There must be hundreds of dollars in gold and silver chalices, I'm thinking.

"What are you doing?"

I swing around, my arms in the air still bent from prying the tabernacle doors. Kiley is halfway down the main aisle, running. I never heard the bastard come in.

"Who are you?"

I can't talk. All the metal zippers and buttons on my jacket are shining from the candlelight in the sacristy, but he can't see me. My face is in the shadows. My white scarf, though, is a dead give-away. I want to disappear into nothing. I want the miracle of Christ rising into the clouds, like I saw so many times in school books. Instead, I must stand here like the priest when he turns to bless the people.

Maybe he's scared, I think. Maybe I should put on the cap and make a move like I'm going to kill him or something. Maybe he'd run.

"What are you doing here? Who are you?"

He is at the altar railing now. He is wearing the long black cassock with the tiny buttons all the way down to his feet. His surplice is gone. He is in street clothes, and I must make a break for it or I'm dead.

"Come down here. I'm coming to get you."

"Better not, Father. I can kill you. I've got a knife." I reach into my top pocket and flick the blade. He can hear it, see it in the candlelight.

"Are you crazy! This is God's house! You have no business up there. Why don't you come down here where we can talk."

He takes a few more steps. "Move back, Father!"

"Put that knife away. Are you mad?"

"Get out of my way, Kiley."

"Father Kiley. So, you know me? You're Catholic, aren't you? Surely this is all some mistake. Come on, son. Put that away. Come, let us talk."

And he jumps me, pulls the knife out of my hand, and begins choking me with the scarf.

"You're a dirty fighter, Kiley," I gasp.

"Just a Mick, son. Southside of Chicago. You bet I am," he says, shoving his knee into my balls.

"You sonofabitch, Kiley," I cry and double up in pain. "You lousy Irishman."

"Who are you? What's your name?"

"None of your fucking business."

"You're from this parish, aren't you?"

"Let me up. I didn't do anything."

"The hell you didn't. You were in the process of robbing God's house!"

He leads me down the steps to the first pew. I'm staring at the Sacred Heart again. I'm avoiding Kiley's face.

"Sit down. Look at me! I can't believe you're Catholic. I can't believe a Catholic would act this way. What's the matter with you? Why would anyone want to *steal* something from Christ, when Christ is all giving? You *are* a Catholic?"

"I was . . . " I reach into my shirt and pull out the holy medals around my neck. "I still wear these to keep the old man and the old lady happy. I even went to school here. I was almost an altar boy once. I still know it. Father Svoboda remembers me. Listen, Father, I'm sorry. I was just goofing around."

"You threatened to kill me! What were you doing up there?"

"Nothing. I just wanted to see the inside of the tabernacle. I always wanted to look inside there. And I just, well, I just felt like doing it finally."

"You were going to steal the chalices, weren't you?"

"I wanted to see one close up, that's all. I wanted to hold it. I wanted to see how it feels in your hand when you drink from it. I used to play priest when I was little; when it was raining outside and there was nothing else to do. I used to fix the dining room table with some candles and make an altar. Then I'd dress up like a priest with anything I could find. Then I'd pretend to say mass."

"Son . . . no, no. You don't do that here. Don't you remember that only priests are allowed to touch these things? To offer the body and blood of Christ in Holy Mass? You don't belong up there. You studied all this in school. You know that. You've committed a mortal sin. Go up to the altar rail, go there before the Blessed Mother, and ask the forgiveness of her

Son. I want you to say the Act of Contrition ten times while I put things in order. Then I'll hear your confession."

Father Kiley disappears into the back of the church while I kneel down at the altar railing and really try to pray for the first time since grammar school. There were times, when you were really praying, when you were really thinking about nothing else but being good, everything being good, everybody, the whole world, and then you stepped outside the church and everything was good, everything was different. I was different. It was something like being in love. It was a wonderful feeling. But you never seemed to be able to keep it that way. Something else would suddenly happen, and you were changed into your old self again. Nothing was good. Maybe the old man changed it because he hollered at me. Or maybe one of the guys wanted to do something, and that was stronger or better or more fun than what you got in praying. To get close to God again, find that feeling again, it seemed you had to keep going back to church; you had to keep trying to find it because it never lasted.

"O my God," I whispered aloud, "I am heartily sorry for having offended Thee, and I detest all my sins, because I have offended Thee, my God, Who art all good and deserving of all my love. I firmly resolve, with the help of Thy grace, to confess my sins, to do penance, and to amend my life. Amen."

I said the Act of Contrition more than ten times. I said some Our Fathers and some Hail Mary's too. I knew Father Kiley was kneeling a few pews behind me.

"Do you want me to hear your confession now?" he whispered.

"No, not now, Father. I'd like to go home, please. I'm sorry, Father."

"Would you like to just talk awhile?"

I shook my head no.

"Come visit me soon at the priest's house, will you? There will be privacy for us to talk. Will you do that?"

"Yes, Father. I'm really sorry, Father. Thank you."

He ushered me out the front doors of the church. At the curb, two squadrons of police waited for me.

I simply confessed everything to a private dick at the local police station. I told him I was going to rob the church. I told him about the chalices, peddling them for some good dough on Maxwell Street, I told him that I didn't really need the dough and that when it came right down to it I don't know why I did it except that it seemed exciting. But he still wasn't happy. Once they get you, these bastards, they expect you to confess to everything. Every crime they've never been able to solve.

"Who else you work with?"

"Nobody. Just me."

"You know John Mladic?"

"I don't remember."

"He remembers you. He says you used to steal a lot of cars together. He's still doing time at St. Charles, you know."

"I think maybe I met him once."

"Quit shittin' me. He's your buddy!"

"I got a lot of friends. What else you want from me?"

"I want some names. Or else your ass'll be in a sling. Make it easier for yourself in Boy's Court."

· I gave him nothing. I told him what I did and that was it. There are certain things you just don't do, like squeal on your friends.

There was a knock on the door and then some shadows behind the frosted glass. The dick got up, opened the door a little, mumbled something, then opened it wide. "Come in," he said.

First Kiley walked in. Then my old man.

"Hello, Father," the dick said. "Take a chair over there, Father." My old man he left standing.

"Well, the boy says he didn't do anything, Father. I mean, thanks to you, he didn't do anything. He wanted the chalices all right. He says he hasn't been involved in anything else, but I don't believe him. Who can believe a thief? Even his buddies say it ain't so."

"Son," Kiley held my shoulder, "you did wrong, so tell the man everything. Wipe your conscience clear of all this. If you've committed other crimes, tell the officer this. There's no reason to protect anyone else. Laws have been broken against man, against God. We are here to see that these laws are upheld. It's this man's duty to seek the truth. It's my duty as well. Help us. You will find God is forgiving."

"Fuck you, Father."

The dick pushed me against the wall, held me there with his elbow against my throat. My old man said something to me in his language, but I ignored him.

"Here," the dick shouted to the old man and pointed. "Sit down here."

Kiley whispered something to the dick. Another cop came in. The three of them began whispering and nodding their heads while the old man and me stared at each other. Then everyone disappeared but the old man and Kiley.

"Why you do this?" the old man asked.

I just shook my head.

"Listen to your father!" Kiley shouted. "He cares about you. He wants to help."

"You don't know my father."

"You no good," says the old man. "Me work hard and son bum, all the time out never home. Never help work. Never help house. Never church, all the time out."

"You don't know what the hell you're talking about."

And the old man got up, walked over to me, and swung his fist into the side of my head.

"Goddam you!" I screamed, pushing him into Kiley.

Kiley quickly separated us, comforting the old man, sitting him in the chair.

"Listen, the both of you," he pleaded. "You can't do this to each other. I've never seen this before between a father and son. You've got to come together. You're both acting like children. Act like men!"

I didn't answer him. The old man kept shaking his head, talking to himself in another language.

"Listen to me, son. I want to hear your confession now, right here before I leave or else you'll be spending the next six months in St. Charles Reformatory. Do you understand that? St. Charles! You're going to be put away, locked up with all the other young hoods who rob and fight and are destined to live a life of crime — murder, rape, prison, death. Are you on that road too? Is that the way to make a name for yourself? Answer me, goddamn it!"

"No. No, Father."

Then I heard this terrible hacking sound like a man trying to clear his nose by sucking it all back inside his mouth. I looked at the old man, and his face just crumbled. He was crying out loud and saying the word "jail" over and over to himself.

Father Kiley gently held him by the shoulder and walked him out of the room. It was the nicest thing I ever saw anyone do to the old man, holding him across the back like that, helping him. You just didn't do that to him. The old lady didn't. I didn't.

I never saw him cry before. Never. He was made to make other people cry, like the old lady. I saw him come close to killing her with a bread knife once. When I was little, I took some money from his pocket, and he waited till I sat down for supper and I reached for the food. Then he came down on my hand with the lid handle of the old cook stove, smashing my fingers. I remember screaming in pain, watching the blood web across my clean plate while the old lady said nothing and kept eating all the while.

He was easy to hate.

But now he was old and crying and began to make me cry. I wanted to run up and hold him the way Father Kiley did. The way I did when I was little and sometimes on Saturdays he would take me to the icehouse where he worked and show me how ice was made, chipping off splinters for me to suck smooth.

And just look at us now, I wanted to shout. A hell of a bunch of Magyars, crying like babies. But I didn't say anything. I turned away so no one could see what was happening to me. Let them see the old Magyar cry, not me. Crying's for women, for Serbs like the old lady. It's good for them, he used to say. It cleans them out. Keeps them pure. Women should cry all the time. But for men — it leads to madness.

Kiley closed the door and sat next to me. "Are you ready?"

I knelt on the floor and covered my face with my hands. "Bless me, Father, my last confession was three or four years ago. I've missed Sunday mass many times. I have not honored my father and mother. I've lied to them, hated them, disowned them. I've destroyed things at school. I've cheated, I've taken the name of God in vain many times. I've stolen things. I've even tried to rob a church. I've touched myself. I've touched many girls. I can't seem to stop this. And I don't feel bad about it, about a lot of these things. I just seem to do them, Father, and never think about wrong."

"Why? How can you explain this?"

"I can't. I don't know."

"Doesn't the thought of eternal hell bother you?"

"No. I can't believe it. I don't seem to be afraid of anything anymore. It's almost like I enjoy being afraid. I want that, more of it, but I can't explain it, Father. Why do I feel this way? I hate work, what it's done to my old man, my old lady. Why do I want to screw every good looking broad I see? Why do I sometimes think there would be nothing to killing someone? And why do I feel so great when I'm doing these things or wanting to do them? Why, Father? Why? I want to do everything everybody else says I can't do. Is that a good confession, Father? And right now I'm afraid, and I feel good about it. How do you explain that? I'm afraid of jail, of what could happen to me there. I want to be better than I am. I want the truth, too, Father. Just like you. Just like the cops. I want to begin again, Father. I'm sorry. I'm sorry, Father. I'm sorry about the old man. Bless me, Father . . ."

29

In the end, I was free. Never prosecuted, never jailed. Later I understood what a good guy Father Kiley was. How he managed to make the cops drop the case. How he made the old man kick in $50 to keep the local newspaper out of the mess, our names clean.

I confess: it worked. Father Kiley, the old man, both of them saved me from a life of crime.

Hassock, you're a sucker for irony. Who did you steal that from, Chekhov? Well, thank God that's over.

For a beginning I would forget the past and become a teacher myself.

Now isn't that a hell of a way to go on with the story? Why should anyone care what happened to a man with an opening like that? Christ, you can do better.

To tell you the truth, I'm lost for the moment. Looking, as usual, for an opening, a place to begin.

Hassock, just tell the goddam story, will you? No excuses.

If there were enough art to my storytelling, I could somehow fade from that criminal past to the virtuous choice of the present and really make you believe that the kind of kid just described could become, quite naturally, a teacher.

How could a kid like that ever get through high school? Well, he did. He had the brains. And more than that. Given the right teacher, he could become anything. The trouble was, as he said, he very seldom had any teachers who were worth a shit.

How many teachers, really, mattered in your life? How many high school teachers do you remember this very moment? Remember them because they brought about some significant change in you?

Fortunately, he had two: the fag, Castrati, and the Jew, Moss.

Castrati had one hell of an influence upon him. First, because he felt so sorry for the sonofabitch; and second because, in a way, he could get close to him. Not in a faggy way. Just close to him in his way of teaching so that you learned because he cared about you.

Moss wasn't like that. You kept your distance with Moss. With him it was something else. With him it was something about what he taught and the way he taught. You had a feeling he was on your side against everything that was wrong, that was unfair, and he would not only let you blow up the school but even show you where to plant the bombs.

Castrati once told him: "You would make a good teacher."

"Me? Come on."

"People interest you. Human beings."

I didn't know what the hell he was getting at. I figured it was just Castrati again, trying to put on the make as usual. With Moss, though, when I graduated from high school and went back there to tell him I was going to junior college and was thinking of becoming a teacher, he didn't even look at me. He was hunched over the bottom drawer of his desk looking for paper clips.

"What the hell do you want to be a teacher for?"

"I'm not sure. Castrati thinks I'd be a good one."

"Castrati? What the hell does he know? All he's in it for is to be close to little boys and spread his half-baked, half-ass philosophy of 'This I Believe.' He's a fucking Boy Scout."

"I got accepted at the junior college on probation. I guess it all depends on how my grades are before I decide anything. I could flunk out and be back where I started from."

"Read everything. That's all. Just read. Can't even find one goddam paper clip in here."

"Maybe I'll major in history."

"What for? History's all bunk. Didn't I teach you that? Here's one. The goddam thing is bent."

"I still like it."

"That's not good enough. You don't just *like* something and decide to spend your whole life with it. That's why so many married people are unhappy."

"You got me interested in it."

"Thanks. I'm sorry. But it's the subject, not the man. I am what I am, and I teach what I am. Do you understand what the hell I'm talking about? And I'm only one man. You're going to have to put up with a lot of boredom in the classroom. It's all agony, agony."

"I'll just have to wait and see."

"Be a plumber. Learn a trade. Isn't that what they tell you in this high school? This is a neighborhood of foreigners and greenhorns. Work in the factories. Make money. Save. Buy a house. Get married. Raise a family. Be a success. Send your kids here someday. With luck, I'll be dead. So go be a plumber. There's no money in history. My brother, now, my brother, Harry. He sells linoleum. There's a success story for you. There's a job. Sell linoleum. Be a linoleum cutter. Tile. Tile's good too. Learn to set tile. It's the coming thing."

That's Moss. A great guy. Moss, if you're out there, I hope the hell you understand what happened to me. I know the bastards gave it to you in the end. I read Miller's "The Crucible" after it was all over. I know those fuckers got you for teaching communism. I know you suffered in the '50's. Fuck them, Moss. I loved you. And you were right about Lincoln and all

31

those goddam Indians.

Hassock, fuck the Indians and get on with the story, will you?

Where was I? Again, if this story were to be a true work of art (which I originally intended it to be) I should be merely suggesting these influences upon the kid. Why suggest? Castrati and Moss were the two most important reasons I became a teacher. The other thing I'll try to get to now. This business of the crime. And, if you will, the redemption . . . second-birth, whatever it's called.

After the incident with the cops, Kiley, and the old man, I just gave up the fun of being a hood. That's all there's to it. The desire or whatever was gone. I've thought about it many times. I've tried to pinpoint the precise moment, reason, why a kid so bad should suddenly turn good, and damn it I'm confused.

And don't any of you half-ass social workers, nice-guy cops, and loving holy priests out there start patting yourselves on the back. Sure you had something to do with it, but you were not the whole thing. Not at all.

I confess: I was scared. Maybe deep down, all the brainwashing of the church about punishment really worked. But just the threat of jail isn't going to end the threat for everyone. I knew guys who had been sent to St. Charles and other juvenile homes. I saw them come back tougher than ever — cigarette smokers when they went in, dopers when they got out; shoplifters when they went in, armed robbers when they got out; straight when they went in, queers when they got out.

So I was scared of what I might turn into. That, and of course, the old man. The old man crying. Sure we had fights right up to his very death. But we also had better times. I drank with him. I slowly tried using the old language again. I took better care of the old lady. I gave them both money whenever I could. I visited the relatives with them.

We laughed and hollered and swore and talked about everyone else. We listened to the Slavic Hour over the radio, and the old lady sang to herself while the old man kept time with his foot. Years later I would come back to visit them in the bungalow in Chicago, and we would play pinochle throughout the night.

I don't think the old man ever understood why I taught for a living. Man's work was with his hands. In time, the old lady seemed to forget who I was. I think the old man would have been happier had I become a tool and diemaker like my cousin Holub. Yet he was impressed that I wore a white shirt to work, and he often called me "professor" jokingly.

We never talked about my past. That happened to somebody else's son. Not his. While I was in Europe, he had the old lady committed to the crazy house. She once sat on the corner fireplug holding a red umbrella for three days and three nights. He was embarrassed. He locked her in the basement after that. But she set fire to the house.

The way the mind can change so fast. How inconceivable. We never know what we might become.

I was somebody else. I wore a crewcut, white buck shoes. I turned into Joe College one day. I held books in my arms, tight against my body. I held them like I really believed in them, really felt they held the secret to what I wanted to be, what might become of me. At times, if I thought about it too much, I became afraid and wondered all about myself.

Once, as Joe College, I saw the image in a mirror and didn't recognize myself. Starting with the hair, moving to the eyebrows, the eyes, the nose, the lips, the mouth, the neck, the chin . . . who was this? The more I looked, the more frightening it became. I began seeing beyond the eyes. I began to turn into silver, into light.

And once in junior college I was playing a game of pool with some friends from a Psych class. Suddenly the green felt table, the cue stick, the blue chalk, the rack, the colored balls . . . everything began to mix, to whirl. Into it all floated the guys from the gang, the old man and old lady, Kiley, the cops, Moss, Castrati.

Was I here? Was I playing pool again with the guys at Windy City? Were we going out for a joyride later? Were the broads waiting? Was I going to get some titty? Who's got some dough? Should we find a drunk to roll?

Memory . . . mind . . . I can't make it all work. It won't hold anything still. The family . . . there's a history of insanity. The old lady's mother. Didn't she kill one of her own children? Didn't an uncle hang himself in the garage? What about me? What's my name?

"Jesus!"

"What?"

"You win again. You must have been born and raised in a pool hall. How about another game of 8-ball?"

"No. Let's go. I've got some work to do."

This has happened to me before, losing control. Usually I get it back, everything in order, in a day or two. The first time I was just a little kid. It happened around Lent, just before Easter. I was fasting more than the priests called for. I was feeling very good. I woke up the night of Good Friday and saw Christ on the cross at the foot of my bed. For a long time he stayed there, and the whole room glowed like gold.

I was too scared to ever tell anyone about it.

I just started touching everything, talking to more people, being with more people, doing more things till everything went back in place again.

It was when I got too alone with myself that these things could happen.

After the pool hall incident I began to pray again. I was afraid of what the mind could do all by itself. I sought the help, the traditions of the old church to put order into my life.

For a moment, I even turned to Norman Vincent Peale's, THE POWER OF POSITIVE THINKING.

In a matter of days, my life was normal once again. I still prayed once in a while, but seldom went to church. I was enjoying junior college. I was enjoying ideas.

Rita disappeared from my life. I would see her occasionally with her girl friends. She would wave and sometimes kid my about my white bucks — fruit boots, she called them. I never touched her again, except in my imagination.

I can barely imagine what I'm about to tell you next.

I keep stalling here at the typewriter.

Keep looking out the windows, watching the wind move the last leaves on the birch trees.

I hear the first flock of geese flying overhead, arrowing their way through the sky toward the marsh many miles south of here.

I feel like painting some watercolors now, before getting on with the end of this part of the story. I look forward to that. I haven't felt the real beginning of that yet.

I'm anxious to find where my mind will take me.

I was thinking last night, when the wind awoke me, that maybe it's time to go to the old country. Maybe as soon as I get to the end of all this I'll get dressed and try Prague or Budapest. In a way, that's where I started from, and I'm almost afraid to go back.

Tell them your real name, Hassock: Blazen, Miroslav Blazen. Bohemian, Hungarian, Croation, everything. Tell them how you changed it to Hassock because it seemed more comfortable and was harder to forget. You don't want immortality. Not much, eh Hassock?

I'm Miroslav Blazen by birth. Miro, they sometimes call me. Now where the hell's that tube of Prussian blue?

After two years of junior college, I finished the required courses at a downstate university, though not immediately. I had a number of odd jobs in between. In time I amassed the proper number of credit hours in education for certification and was eventually channeled into my first teaching job by the Placement Bureau of the university.

"There's an opening for an English teacher on the outskirts of Chicago," the director of teacher placement said. "You would be fairly close to home. Campbell City is an industrial area. Railroads, trucking, a bulldozer plant there. Good tax base. A mixed community. People interested in seeing their kids get the education denied them. They want the best and support the schools to the hilt. Good adult education program too. Trades, business courses, remedial English. You might even work yourself into that program eventually and make yourself some extra money. Never hurts, right? Two high schools: Campbell City East and Campbell City West. West's a little more middle class, some upper middle as well. You'll be at East. $3,500 to start. I'd take it if I were you."

I took it for reasons I was unable to explain at the time. Or afraid to examine. I took it because the superintendent of East Campbell City High appeared to be a nice guy. I took it because the school itself, the "plant" as they referred to it, was brand new. I never saw a new school building where I came from. I always thought that schools were just there, forever, like streets and sidewalks.

But East Campbell City High was all glass and patios. Sunlight. The outside was inside. A perfect setting to teach. I took the job to experience that. And I took it because the chairman of the department was a man, a good man, who would probably be easier to work for than some frustrated spinster. I recalled all the women teachers I ever had, all of them such a pain in the ass. And I was still young enough to feel the inevitable conflicts because of the difference in age.

Most importantly, I took the job because I was just married and on my way to becoming a responsible adult.

But I didn't do all the things that were expected of me. I didn't live in the community where I taught, as the superintendent had suggested. I decided to live in Chicago instead. My wife, a downstate girl, was anxious to live and work in the city. And I was willing to be seduced by all the attractions of city life, especially Chicago at night.

We found an apartment on the Northside near the expressway, which would quickly get me to school. Betty was able to catch a bus only a block away and arrive at the bank where she worked in less than 20 minutes.

The drive to Campbell City was a long one — almost 40 miles a day round trip. I left very early each morning yet the school day itself was short; the administration saw to it that my afternoon obligations were few, since I traveled such a great distance.

Is that a compound sentence, Hassock? What kind of sentence structure is that? Let's see you diagram that, Teach.

No one was more surprised about my new profession than I.

Than "I?" English has gone to your head, Hassock.

Oh, I had talked to Castrati and Moss about it years before, yet I didn't really believe I would make it. For one thing, I have never been comfortable around people. How could I handle an entire classroom? How could I be part of a faculty?

I turned to teaching I guess because there was some kind of respect attached to it. It was better than anything my father was, better than anything anyone in the neighborhood was. Nobody in the family, none of the fathers of my friends, had ever worn a suit to work. Most of them would probably never in their lives be addressed as "Mr." anybody.

I must confess too that I turned to teaching because it seemed safe. Because I was afraid to become anything else. After my black motorcycle days, I sought refuge in the classroom.

What the fuck are you always afraid of, Hassock?

The more I began to experience in the field of education, the more I came to realize that teaching is a haven for cowards of all sorts. Teachers, almost all of them, teach because of a fear of failing to do anything else with their lives. Classrooms all over America are filled with desperation, 90 pound weaklings, bent psyches, bitterness. Second-best yet secure in their resignation. The years go by. Dead wood, dead-heads, immovable objects awaiting a state pension and an early retirement.

And I was as guilty as they. I was preparing to play house and set-up a teaching way of life. I may have had other ambitions, perhaps artistic leanings. But I turned to — or fell back on — teaching, at least for a beginning — the common excuse (illusion) of all teachers till it's too late.

If you're still looking for a story, suspense, there isn't any yet. There may not be for a while. Stay with me till the end. I am telling a very simple story, a very simple plot: how I became what I am at the moment. Our story.

Oh, Hassock, that's neat. Did you learn that from Ellison's, INVISIBLE MAN?

East Campbell City High School gave me all the customary experiences of a new teacher: excitement, fear, elation, depression. Plus overcrowded classrooms, club assignments, guard duty in the halls, dance supervision, study hall monitoring, and five classes of English.

Classes at Campbell City East were not really grouped according to abilities as they were at Campbell City West and other upper middle-income suburban high schools.

Oddly enough there was too much local pressure against such discrimination. The working people of the community generally understood democracy and were against any division of kids into smart and dumb

36

whatever the educators might advocate for the good of all students. Class distinction, intellectual capabilities *was* democracy to the modern educator.

Actually, now that I think about it, people usually get the schools and teachers they deserve. An unconcerned community gets unconcerned schools, unconcerned administrators, unconcerned teachers, and a school board that functions according to what was good enough for them in their days. An involved community gets the best of everything, including a school board that veers slightly to the right.

Don't tell me that big business, economics, runs the schools, too, Hassock?

Everyone was in the same boat at Campbell City East except that the smarter kids were given more busy work. The administration felt this was the best way to handle the situation even though, in time, the smart ones would appear as dumb as the rest.

At the senior level there was some underhanded work going on. A few teachers in English, math, science, and history felt that there were enough kids of college potential to create a sort of advanced section in each area and encouraged them into these areas. It worked occasionally. Eventually administrators and parents would tangle about the whole scheme being undemocratic and then the whole system would be dismantled, only to slowly reassemble again.

Significantly, though, new teachers were never given a crack at working with advanced students. Apprenticeship had to be served with the average and below average. Sometimes an IQ of 120 or better would be tossed in — mistakenly.

The first words I ever spoke in a classroom were: "Would you please be quiet?" Later I would resort to, "Shut up!" And years later I developed even better openers for attention.

Hey, Hassock, how come you're the only Indian with a mustache?

I began not really knowing what would become of me in the classroom. Unaware of who I was or what was expected of me, I came prepared to give them kindness, humor, maybe even something like love. An atmosphere for learning.

That's cute, Hassock. Did you learn that in one of your education courses?

In a life short enough in time but strange enough in experience, I felt I knew a little as to what it might be all about.

What?

"Toughness," a pose I had shed with my past, I was advised by college educators to adopt an attitude of strictness. And so I began my act.

This I gotta see.

But those plans I spoke of in the beginning. First, to take a look at those.

Part I Self-Conflict (not prepared for responsibilities?)

Parts I & II
—Teaching as a cowardly act
—A safe way out? In?

In Parts I & II . . . teaching a rebound from
something feared. (Is this *clear*?)

Part I

Part II Breakdown

SETTING
—small industrial town west of Chicago
—dictates what is right
—teacher as actor living in the fantasy
of always being someone/thing else?

STYLE
—awkward
—good/bad
—boring

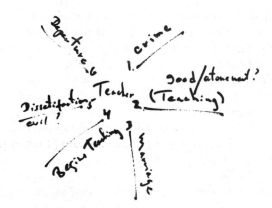

Jesus Christ, Hassock, you mean this is only Part I of a mystical 3-part

series?

I entered room 131 each day carrying my imitation leather attache case. In it I carried all my books, all my lesson plans, all the names of the students I would have to live with for the year. I carried supplies as well: paper clips, red pencils, scotch tape, chalk, manila folders, rubber bands, ball point pens, erasers, and a stapler.

Only the hand that erases writes the true thing, eh Hassock?

I kept everything neat, everything in place. Whenever I was not working from the case — grading papers, going over lesson plans, checking seating charts — I kept it locked.

My clothing was practical. Always a white shirt, a striped tie, and one $45 department store suit with the jacket a reversible sport coat for versatility. My white bucks remained in the closet for after school loafing. Instead I wore a pair of wing-tipped black oxfords. All that remained of my college days was a crewcut. I looked younger than my years. I carried the attache case with me at all times, not to be mistaken for a student.

The bell rang and half the class was gawking out the window while the other half stood in little clusters, sneaking glances at me, whispering, laughing. One girl began applying her makeup. A tall, tough looking Mexican kid slicked back his hair in duck-assed fashion using a rat-tailed comb.

"Would you please be quiet?" I heard myself say.

Noise and confusion continued. "Please be quiet and be seated!" I yelled.

The voice registered. They took their seats, but not without making faces to one another, signaling that the teacher before them looked like he was going to be a hard-nosed bastard. I knew exactly what they were thinking, all the hell that lay ahead of me.

'Lie' or 'lay,' Hassock? What's the proper form, Teach?

I was nervous. And as I began to talk I found myself pacing the front of the classroom. I could neither use the lectern not sit comfortably behind the desk. My voice was unsteady, continually wavering in pitch. For all my teacher training hours in public speaking, I could not look a one of them in the eye.

"As I call out your names, please take the following seats in alphabetical order: Anderson, the first desk there by the window, Bess, right behind him, Brenner, Caine, Frazer, Higgins, Hummel, Judson, Koch . . . " Deep laughter erupted in the classroom. "Knock it off!" I yelled. "Is it pronounced Coke or Cock?" I asked. "Cock," a forced high voice squealed from the back of the room.

39

"Sucker," somebody else added.

"Coke," a small, pimply-faced girl whispered in front of me.

"Thank you. Lamar . . ."

Thirty-one kids in my junior English class and not enough desks. While one student remains standing, two more come in as transfers, immediately recognized by the others. Groans of "Oh, no!" and hand gestures welcome them. That makes thirty-three, three of them standing at the back of the room because there are not enough desks.

"I'll have desks for you by tomorrow. For the time being squeeze in with one of your friends." Chaos. Kids pushing each other off the seats, one guy yelling, "Hey, I got room for only half a cheek!"

"Quiet! Quiet! Please. I'm Mr. B. Just call me that. This is English III, room 131, 1st hour. Check your programs to see if you have all of that information, otherwise you don't belong here." One kid gets up and walks out amidst laughter, whistling, and clapping.

"Okay. That's enough. Do you all have copies of *Adventures in American Literature*? Good. Be sure to bring them to class with you every day. From tomorrow on there'll be no excuse for not having the proper book in class. That goes for paper, pen, pencils, and assignments as well. No excuses to the locker, and no passes to the washroom except in extreme cases of emergency. You're juniors now. Next year you'll be upper-classmen. I expect you to be responsible to yourselves and to me."

"What if you have to go real bad?"

"I don't think that's funny, buddy. The next time you have a question like that, raise your hand. Or better yet, come up to the desk and ask me properly. I'll determine how necessary it is."

Already I could hear myself sounding like a smart-ass. Like all the teachers I despised. Here it was now inside of me. I hated it.

Now you're talking, Hassock. When the hell you going to be yourself?

They looked at me with hate. Slowly I tried to regain some of the ground I lost. I spoke softly. I tried a little humor. I smiled. I wanted to be liked, to be a good teacher. I could see myself out there in Maaze's class getting the big finger ready.

"This is an interesting course. I think you will like it, profit from it. We're going to read some good stories, articles, essays, even some poetry." The groaning began with the mention of poetry.

"It isn't that bad. You'll see. I used to hate poetry myself. I really did. All that pansy stuff about clouds and flowers and love . . . all the things the old maid school teachers try to stuff into you." This broke them up. I was getting through. I had no plans whatsoever to say anything about what we would be learning and certainly no desire to fight them about poetry. I was just talking out my nervousness and had somehow caught their attention. And it would take me years to learn the lesson I had just unconsciously taught.

The remainder of the hour was a carefree give-and-take. The bell rang, and we parted with some friendliness, understanding, and a touch of uncertainty. "He's all right." "He's kind of nice." "At least he's better than that bitch we had last year." "He seems a little crazy." "We'll see . . ." echoed from the bunch of them crowding through the doorway.

Hassock! Hassock! Quit scratching those mosquito bites on your ass and take a break or something. The drama in this story leaves a person breathless. Go talk to the sunflowers or something. Tell us a story about that artist friend of yours in New Mexico. No, not the one who starved herself to death and was crucified by the Penitenties. That sounds too much like theme. Tell us about Arroyo L., the high school art teacher. The guy you taught Henry Miller to, remember? An artist, no less, and you had to start him off with Henry Miller. And then he ups and shows you, leaves the art room, the whole damn teaching scene one morning to find himself in New Mexico, putting the final touches to his own merry-go-round. How many people have you done this to, Hassock? How many did you teach to live a life you're afraid to lead? Is that what a teacher does? Tell us about the big blackboard you set up in the woods; the clearing you made the other day for the merry-go-round Arroyo said he would ship to you. Show us the poem you put on the blackboard in anticipation. Hurry, before you erase it.

For EVERYTHING under the SUN
Introducing, Arroyo L. of New Mexico
NU-MOHK-MUCK-A-NAH!

sunshine on his electric stick

He's a Doctor of Box Candy
A merry-go-round in a Garage
A visit to a Ballet Class
A circus of the Mind
A time of snow
WHY DELAY THE DREAM?

"Please touch" is the plea
CAN WORDS ALONE STILL MAKE A PLAY?
"I want some space to put my life in order" — the Dilemma of the Magic Revolutionary

Looking over some of my attempts to begin this story, I notice I was going to say at this point: "I remained pretty much a loner at East Campbell City High."

That should be obvious by now. I have trouble with most people. Unless an honesty is evident between us, I find a friendship impossible to

41

begin. A confession, of sorts, before anything can happen. Which takes time.

So I stayed clear of most of the other teachers in the beginning — and even more so in the end. There was a teacher's lounge where everyone would gather during free periods. I would dodge into there for a quick smoke, nod hello to the strange faces, and usually leave within a few minutes. I overheard the usual teacher talk — grading papers, good and bad students, salaries, P.T.A., administrators, vacations, study halls, criticism of other teachers — but I never joined in the discussion.

Then Ted Schauk came up to me one day, forced a cigar in my mouth, and made me listen to him. The more involved I got with the kids, the more personal problems and anxieties I began to develop, the more I sought the company and words of Ted Schauk.

He could always be found in the lounge before school, after school, any free time he had. He was a smoker — cigars, cigarettes, and most often a bulldog pipe that had worked its way into a favorite niche in his mouth.

We talked books, we talked writers, we talked world affairs. Schauk had hundreds of stories about the people of Campbell City: the politicians, the clergy, the businessmen, the police. As for students, no matter whom I mentioned Schauk either had the same kid, or a brother, a sister, and sometimes even the parent years ago.

"You think Higgens is bad," he would start out. "You should have had the older brother. Now there was a worthless bastard. He threw a wrench at me once. He wanted to be an automobile mechanic, and he used to drag this tool box with him to class all the time. I told him to leave it in shop or his locker and finally I pushed it out into the hall. After class he went to get it and threw a wrench at me. Now he's a mechanic on the westside. Terrible family. The parents are separated. The old man works for the railroad when he's sober. The old lady moved in with some hillbilly."

He had the history of everybody, and I enjoyed listening to him as he told his stories about teaching with warmth, wit, and often deep concern.

When there were particular gripes about school policy (like the unwritten law requiring teachers to be "stationed" in their classrooms 20 minutes before the first hour bell) he would usually agree with me how asinine it all was, then relate a 30 minute monologue on the stupidity of administrators, including a confession of how he learned to smile, say "yes," and then bend school policy to suit his own pleasure.

"But you've got to remember, they don't bother people like me. You're the new breed. You've been taught by professionals. You've had all the education courses about school and community relations. I've been here too long. I have tenure, you see. I'm safe. But you're not. So watch your ass. They have to get me on a morals charge or kill me before they can empty my desk."

Is this all according to plan, Hassock? Where the hell are you? Are you coming to the part where you begin to hate your work? Do you really doubt you're a teacher after all?

I taught for three months with little to moderate success. I was beginning to think of other things to do. I seriously questioned my role as a teacher. Not that I felt I couldn't become a good one in time. I wondered about the value of it all. Eighty percent of the kids were absolute bastards. Hopeless. And the more I listened to other teachers, the more I studied the makeup of Campbell City, the more I read, the more I had to meet the handful of parents that showed up for P.T.A., the more discouraged I became.

What the hell kind of an effect could one man have in a kid's life? How could I possibly help a kid to overcome the handicap of idiot parents, a half-ass community more interested in basketball than books, and all the rotten kids who would continue to drag down the aspirations of any kid trying to get a little bit above the rest of them?

Sure, look who's talking. Look where I came from. Yet I managed to survive. Why me and not them? What were the variables; their lives were destined for major and minor disasters. They would drop out of school as soon as they were of age. They'd join the services. The broads would get knocked up and be married before they ever heard of Hawthorne.

I talked literature to them, and they would look at sex magazines, hot rod books, and carry on a continual correspondence behind my back, or more often, right in front of me.

> Dear Sweetheart,
> *Hon* I didn't get a letter from you today.
> Have you been working that hard. I try my best to write
> you everyday and so far I think I only missed one day
> so far. I told you *honey* I love to read your letters. My mother
> write more than you *hon.* Who am I gonna marry you or her.
> *Hon* as soon as I know I can marry you I coming hom. But I Have
> to know. But I guess they won't signe for you. *Hon* the chaplain
> said he would marry us but I would much rather see your
> parents at the wedding. If they don't signe for you before I go
> Over-Seas I'm going awol and take you somewhere where I
> can marry you and I mean it. *Hon* I'm sorry but I have to go.
> I'll write more tomorow.
> > Love,
> > > Jack P.S. I love you hon. Please

marrie me please.

You

&

me

Hi Sweetheart,

I'm in Mr. B's class now, I'm gonna try to write
to you, there's nothing to talk about. Oh yea! didn't I tell
you not to call other guys? How come you called Hank? I'm
sorry but I don't trust anyone, I just don't want to loose you . .
that's all! So try not to call other guys. OK?

Yea! I guess I must have gave you that hickey such soft skin
you don't have to try. Oh! When we go over to Joe's Sat. don't
put matches in your bra . . . unless I get to take them out —
answer! What you have fills it nicely.

OK? Just think if you would have got to *hot* we might have
had a little fire going. ha! ha!

Well, I guess I was sort of busy at the time. I'm glad that you
are glad that I was busy at the time (Figure that out) Well I
better go, I'll see you at lunch. GOD!!! that's a long time. I
miss you!!!!!!!!!!!!!!

Love ya eternally,

Bye Bye-e-e-e-e-e Ted

*Hassock, this is the same old bullshit every half-ass teacher tries to write
about. You were going to write something new and honest about teaching.
We know there are kids that can't be taught. You try to make them speak
properly and once they leave the classroom they speak the same as they
always do. Force them to do homework, threaten them. They lie, they cheat,
they brown-nose. They shit all over you at first chance. A few good ones in
the bunch, but never enough to make a difference, right Hassock? No one
really likes to go to school, right Hassock? Everyone would rather fuck
around. Tell us something new, Hassock.*

The last class of the day can destroy you for the afternoon, the night,
the next day, and sometimes for many days to follow. They storm into the
classroom, wearing or holding their jackets and coats and caps, as if the
last hour were merely free time to prepare for the final bell.

It takes me at least 10 minutes every day to get the class in a reason-
able state of calm, but always there is a lower level of talking, whispering,
grinning, note-passing, page shuffling. Little distractions almost impossible to control.

"Open your grammar books to page 139 and take out the diagrams I
assigned. Quietly!"

More noise. More shuffling of papers, more side glances, smiles, obscene gestures. These were older kids, seniors who would be graduating soon and finding employment in the outside world. They had a terrible time writing a decent sentence, constructing a paragraph, spelling a word. For weeks I had been reviewing sentence structure for them, explaining things they had been taught the year before, and the year before that. Grammar, I discovered, is the accumulation of ignorance. They still wrote sentence fragments. They still had difficulty identifying the parts of speech.

"Ed Cass, Betsy Lobar, please put sentences 3 and 5 on the board."

"I don't have that one," Ed chuckles, looking for support from his friends.

"What do you mean, you don't have it?"

"I don't have it." He smiles again, satisfied with himself, with his buddies mumbling encouragement under their breath.

"Sue Long, take the third sentence please."

"I didn't get a chance to finish my English last night."

"What do you mean, 'finish'? That's the first sentence!"

"I mean I had too much other homework to do."

I called on seven other people. Nobody had the work. They were all prepared to copy down whatever somebody else put on the blackboard.

"Let's take a look at Betsy's sentence: Next Sunday I ride the train West."

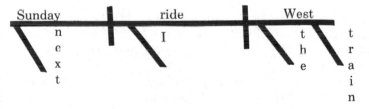

"All right. Check the diagram carefully, those of you, all of you, who failed to do the assignment. Those of you who did it, compare Betsy's diagram to what you have on your own paper. The subject of the sentence, someone? Let's see some hands! Paul?"

"Sunday."

"Is that correct, class?" Silence. "Paul, is that right?"

"That's what's up there," he laughed and the rest of the class joined in.

"I know 'that's what's up there'," I mocked him. "I'm asking if that's correct?"

"How should I know? I didn't do it." More laughter. Girls talking to one another, oblivious to what I was trying to teach; boys, most of them, listening to the rap of mufflers from passing cars. When the hell was the bell going to ring? Goddam, it's Friday! How much more of this grammar shit!

"All right. Close your books. Take out some paper. We're going to have a quiz."

"Auuugh, another one?" "This is the only class I got quizzes in all the time." "So what? You just flunk 'em anyways."

"Quiet! Enough of that complaining. Take down the following sentence and diagram it. You have 10 minutes before I call in the papers: The man across the street drove his car into a post."

"Where?" smirks, laughter, heads turning around.

"It was not my intention to amuse you, though I know almost anything would. Diagram. And hurry. Keep your eyes on your own paper." And Ed Cass puts his eye right up against his paper. Ha, ha, ha. Ed Cass. Real card.

Finally there was something close to silence. This was all I could do to keep them in line. I had to continually test them, threaten them with failure, give them written work of some sort.

I collected the quizzes, briefly glanced through them, and found one correct diagram.

"You're hopeless. All of you."

"Look who's talking." Loud laughter, hand clapping.

"Who said that?" They all pointed to each other and laughed some more.

"Okay, you want to play games? Nobody leaves this classroom when the bell rings."

"Ah, come on! What do you think we are, grammar school kids?"

"You act like them."

"I didn't do anything, Mr. B., honest. My mother's waiting for me."

"Quiet! I'll send you all down to the Dean's for a week's detention."

"Do I have to stay after school, Mr. B.? I did my homework."

"Everybody stays this time. Sorry, Betsy."

"That's not fair. That's the last time I'm doing anything for this class."

"That's not the right attitude, Betsy. I can't make exceptions. Everybody's at fault here one way or another. You didn't pass the quiz either, you know."

"Who did?"

"Never mind."

"Yeah, but I wasn't fooling around. And I did my homework."

"I know that. I'm sorry it has to be this way. Blame your fellow classmates."

"Mr. B., can I go to the washroom?" John Keene asks.

"No. Not now. I'm going to give a homework assignment."

"Afters?"

"No!"

"But I got to go real bad." Laughter.

"For tomorrow I want you to *add* to today's assignment the 25 sentences on page 140."

"25 sentences! 25 sentences!"

"Are you all deaf? Yes, 25 sentences."

Tension, hate, frustration, building and building. The right side of my head begins throbbing with pain. I sit down at my desk and look at the clock. Half the period remains plus the additional 15 or 20 minutes I have promised to hold them for punishment. Punishment for whom? For them? No, me. Would 25 additional sentences teach them anymore about diagramming? What the hell was I doing?

"Yes, Ed?"

"Can I go when the bell rings? I've got to work after school." "Me too, Mr. B." "Yeah, hey! I got to wash the old man's car."

"Hold it down! Everybody just shut up!"

Then the girls begin to band together, quietly at first by raising their hands, then gradually registering their feelings in shrill, overlapping tones . . . "I've got to watch my baby sister after school" . . . "The old lady'll pound lumps on me" . . . "I got a job too, Mr.B. ("Yeah, a blowjob,", one of the boys throws in for the hell of it.") "I'm supposed to see my history teacher or I'll flunk."

"Then flunk," I said. "You're flunking everything anyway, aren't you? What the hell's the difference?"

"Mr. B. swore, did you hear that?" "Shame on Mr. B. . . . I'm tellin'."

"If you people don't shut up and get busy, you'll be here till 5 o'clock."

And then someone passed gas.

"Who the hell farted?" Cass yelled out. We sat there, all of us, in the laughter, the pointing of fingers, the holding of noses. The embarrassment. The stink.

The bell rang and I dismissed the class.

I left the high school behind me that afternoon as if I were escaping it, racing back home to Chicago through the patches of farmland that still clung to the far western outskirts of the city. The closer I came to Chicago, the slower I was forced to drive as more stoplights began to appear, more cars, more buildings, more pedestrians. And all this, to me, was relief. The pressure was back there at East Campbell High.

I would be home before Betty, and I would relax, read for awhile, and perhaps take her to dinner and a movie. We would have a drink or two at home, maybe make love, and then a good Italian restaurant downtown.

There was this new life, new freedom about being in the city again. Michigan Avenue, the beautiful women, the life on the streets, the lights. All this as so much more than what my life had been reduced to inside of a classroom.

Now, the light in the apartment in late afternoon, the sun slicing through the blinds, the dust drifting in the light. A soft and comfortable place to be. I opened a beer, threw off my jacket, shirt, tie, and stretched out on the sofa, taking up Miller's *Tropic of Cancer* where I had left off.

Betty walked in sometime later and seemed surprised to find me half asleep, smiling to myself.

"Did you make supper, Dear?"

"No. It was such a bitch of a day I thought we'd go for some good Italian food and maybe a movie."

"Again? We just went out two nights ago. Can we afford it?"

"Piss on it. We can afford anything to forget a bad day. Come here, I've got something for you."

She threw her coat on the kitchen table, walked over to the sofa, smiled, sat on his stomach, then bent over to kiss him.

"Ugh, you heavy. You break big Indian's stick. Give him rupture," and he began unbuttoning her suit jacket as she stretched out on top of him, kicking off her shoes.

"Ugh, you're beery," she said, darting her tongue into his mouth.

He dropped Miller's book to the floor without any attempt to mark his place. He removed her blouse and bra while she stood up and took off her skirt and slip. In panties and stockings she stood before him as he reached up and cradled her in his lap like a child. She nibbled at his ears and began loosening his belt.

"Miller's right about everything," he whispered in her hair. "What's the sense of work? What the hell am I teaching? A man busts his ass all day when he should be home fucking."

We used each other this way, in an attempt to remove ourselves from the rest of the day. At least, I did. She seemed comletely happy, in many ways ignorant of what my world was, where I came from, and what was happening to me.

She was a downstate Illinois farm girl, a Baptist, a virgin, when I met her working in a small department store in the town I went to college during my last year. Around the time of Addur.

Addur was my college buddy who first introduced me to Miller's work.

I met him near the end of my third year, a few months before I met Betty.

College girls, I discovered, were all so much rah-rah bullshit. No one like a Rita in sight. No one any different. And the guys, the guys I just never understood at all. On top of all this, it was just a halfass farm college to begin with. That was a big part of the problem. So Betty and Addur were different and important in my life there.

Betty was real to me because she was so practical and innocent. Religion was a small problem. I was still Catholic, but I had stopped going to church. To please Betty's parents, I began going to the Baptist church with her each Sunday. But after we married and moved away to Chicago, neither of us went to any church again. Mostly because of me.

I could go into a great detail describing my courtship of Betty, but most of it took place in an old car I bought. On weekends we would head out for the country roads and just drive till a quiet enough scene appeared. There we would park, sometimes picnic, talk and make a very quiet kind of love. "Wait till we get married," was her usual reply to my advances. She was still bothered by sin and society while I never thought much about it anymore.

I honored her beliefs, though. I'm such a nice guy. Even Rita used to say that. We went about as far as two people can go without quite coming off in the usual way. I grew hornier and hornier over this predicament. Marriage seemed inevitable.

Addur came into my life at just the right time. My discovering him on the same campus of such halfass Joe College types was pure fate. What I discovered and began to worship about him was danger. I had not been around people like Addur since my high school days. And in my attempt to forsake the black leather jacket destiny of my early days, I stayed clear of any person, any experience that might lead me back there again. I had really forgotten what it meant to live a bit on the edge of things. And suddenly, Addur — the only one of his kind I had ever come across at the farm college — a dangerous sonofabitch with an incredible mind as well.

What I loved in Addur was much of what was once myself. Addur, just possibly, was what I might have become sooner, given the insight, the chance, the self-assurance.

He came from the Southwest, stood over 6 feet tall, wore cowboy boots and a leather vest at all times. He rolled his own cigarettes, took snuff, smoked marijuana, took peyote, and drank beer and bourbon to excess. His friends back in New Mexico would send him the maryjane and the peyote in aluminum laundry cases.

He spent a minimum amount of time in class and studies. His real interests were literature, philosophy, art and religion. All of his time was devoted to these subjects plus the added stimulation of drink, drugs, and women. He had been married once. He was much older than the average college senior. He lived in an apartment some distance from the college with an art student, Kathy Loomis.

"A true fucking woman," he would describe her. Though I didn't know what the hell he was talking about. "Do you want a reefer?"

"No."

"Ever try it?"

"Back in high school."

"No shit?"

"No shit."

"You don't seem the type."

"I got religion."

"Bull shit. You're one of those secret sonofabitches, aren't you?"

"I've learned."

"Not between us, old man. We tell all. No secrets. Aren't we in this same fucking cow pasture together? How did we get sentenced to time in the Midwest? Tell me, Blazen. I seem to have lost track of the crime."

"On the job training. Teaching, remember?"

"Teaching? Are we really supposed to be teachers when they turn us out of here? I hate teachers. There are no teachers here. They're all ag majors here. Maybe we're supposed to become farmers. Shitkickers, right?"

"Or there's the business world you're going back to."

"Business? Am I a prospective businessman, or am I a fuckoff? A fuckoff, right? This is all a disguise to please the old man. He got me into this corn college, and it's been a good time. His world I can run from here, if I have to. Real estate, for Christ's sake. Any asshole can sell land. And in New Mexico yet? Do you know what a racket that is? I play Babbit when I have to — from the outside. I'll make the perfunctory moves in the business of daily business — suit, tie, attache case, wife, kids, car. Kiss the little woman goodbye on the way to the office each day. Pinch the secretary's ass. Shut the door, answer a few phone calls — then take out my books, my smokes, my paper and pen and continue my plot to destroy the whole structure and escape to the mountains. Escape up here."

"Thus spake Zarathustra?"

"The master's plan."

We were sitting in the kitchen of Addur's apartment right off the town square. He lived above a furniture store — the whole top floor which was once used for storage. Addur had partitioned all the open space to make it somewhat manageable. There was still the feeling of great space about it, though a part of it definitely had the air of a kitchen plus three or four areas that could be used for bedrooms. The entire front, windows facing the street, served as a combination studio and living room. Addur, under the inspiration of Kathy, had just begun to paint — huge canvases. I envied him his passion for doing anything that gave him satisfaction.

Kathy, who had been asleep in one of the bedrooms, joined us.

"I'll make some tea," she said. "Let's sit in the studio."

"How about calling up one of your friends for Miro here," said Addur.

"Who?"

"Somebody who likes to fuck," he laughed.

"You're impossible," she poked him and went back to the kitchen to make a call.

"Listen, really, you don't have to go through all this. I've got work to do anyway. And I'm supposed to see Betty."

"Bullshit. Just stick around. What do you know about Eckhardt?"

"Who?"

"Master Eckhardt."

"Never heard of him."

"Some fucking teacher you're gonna make. Stick close to the old man here, and learn something. Stay out of those cow barns over there."

"You're right. No, I've never heard of Eckhardt. Hesse I know. We've talked about him. *Steppenwolf, Demian, Siddharta.* I never read anything like that before."

"You get your fill of him in one swallow. Now Eckhardt . . ."

"Tell me about him."

And that's how it was between us. Sometimes I would tell him of a book I had just read, but more often than not, he dominated the conversation. He was far ahead of me — reading, comprehending, full of living ideas it would take me years yet to experience.

As for sex, here too imagination of still another kind expressed itself in ways most stimulating to Addur.

When Kathy's friend, Lenore, finally showed up at Addur's apartment that night, I immediately recognized her as one of the most intriguing faces on campus. Though I was going with Betty, planning to marry her, the body, the face, the style of this woman, Lenore, whose name I didn't even know now, haunted many of my days and nights.

Lenore of the black, black hair, black eyes, olive skin, bizarre jewelry and clothes. She stepped into Addur's apartment, and though I knew nothing of witchcraft, I immediately felt this, mixed with passion, in her presence.

We drank and talked a while, smoked some dope, and gradually I began to settle into things, my head in Lenore's lap, telling adventure stories of my life in crime back in the old neighborhood. Lenore, an art major from an upper-middle class suburb north of Chicago, loved my tales of danger, exaggerated, tales I barely remember being part of.

"Why don't you girls do a strip for us," suggested Addur. "I haven't seen a good striptease since Reno."

He put on some music — Bach, of all things — and Kathy immediately stood up, and slowly began peeling off her sweater, jeans, bra, and just stood there undulating in light blue panties.

Lenore, instead of stripping to the music, removed her skirt and blouse, throwing them on me, and proceeded to dance very suggestively in black panties, black bra, and a brass necklace bobbing from tit to tit, bracelets jangling on both arms, and earrings swinging freely.

"Come on, girls, let's paint," said Addur. "Get down here on the newspaper. Let me take off those pants, Love," he said to Kathy, grabbing the elastic and pulling them down. "Miro, you do Lenore. Here, here take this brush. Help yourself to the paints."

"But I can't paint!" I hollered, and the others joined in with their laughter.

Addur began dabbing red and yellow dots on Kathy's tits, squeezing a tube of titanium white into his hands, smearing the paint all over her stomach, her brown pubic hair, and down her thighs. "Turn over," he said, and painted her ass blue. "Wait, wait," he hollered, running to a shelf for a long roll of white paper. "I'm going to make a print of you," he said. "First the front, then the rear. Who the fuck is this Jackson Pollock guy anyway?"

Bach gave way to Mulligan, to Parker, to Brubeck, to Miles Davis.

I rubbed red into Lenore's beautiful but delicate tits, playing with them all the while. I finger-painted a child's sun on her belly, pulled down her pants and stopped right there, kissing the hairs instead, while she urged me to come in.

Kathy jumped on top of me just as I finished, covering my back with tubes of paint, rolling me over so the two of them could work a rainbow of colors across my chest and prick, while Addur howled from the corner.

A man goes a little crazy with such people, in such times. Rising in my own room the next morning, slightly hungover, shakey, somewhat spaced, I looked back upon the night deeply frightened. I had slipped. Addur scared the hell out of me. He, more than anything else, could put me back. I stayed away from him for many months after that. Though I saw Lenore and Kathy occasionally at the Student Union, we never mentioned that night. And I desired Lenore more than any woman I had ever known up till then in my life.

What I did was turn to Betty with even greater love, greater need. She knew what was important for me and just how to proportion love. I was going to marry her, and that would be it. I would teach. We would live in Chicago. I would very likely never see Addur again. Or Lenore. Yet dark, dark nights would come — impossible to describe their rhyme or reason — and I would drop Betty off at her house, then turn the car right around, and stalk the seedy parts of town, frequent a house of prostitution, drink excessively in a working man's bar, then go look for Addur to talk to.

Sounds like Herman Hesse, Hassock. Or are you feigning Dostoevski? Is this supposed to be Crime or Punishment, Hassock? Or maybe confessional literature? You fallen-away Catholics had confession for that. Find thyself a priest, Hassock.

Later that Friday evening Betty and I went to the Milano Restaurant in Chicago. We had a platter of antipasto, pasta and clam sauce, lasagne, and a large bottle of Chianti that knocked us both out.

"I'm fed up with it," I told her. "My first year of teaching, and I've had it up to here."

"It's bound to get better. And you don't have to stay there, you know. Start on your Master's this summer. I'll work. Don't worry. My folks will help out if we need it. When you get your Master's you can look for a better school."

"I'll never get a Master's."

"Why?"

"I just don't think I'll ever get one, I have a feeling, can't explain, I'm finished with education. Here, finish. Drink. Let's go home and make love on the sofa. I love that apartment. Sometimes I don't ever want to leave it."

"You're crazy."

"Only in the morning do I hate the apartment. I hate waking up to it. The early morning darkness. That ugly, old fashioned refrigerator. Those fluorescent lights beside the medicine cabinet. Deadly, fluorescent lights. The last light you see, just before dying, must be fluorescent. In the morning, waking up in that apartment, thinking of teaching, I'm dying, dying in that fluorescent light, that face in the mirror."

"Don't talk that way. What does your department head say about your teaching? He encourages you, doesn't he?"

"He's coming to visit my class again. Any day now. Well, he likes me, if that's what you mean. If that's encouraging. He likes me. The first time he stopped in, I was impressive as hell. That was October. Things have fallen apart since then. They weren't sure of me yet, the kids. I could run a tight ship then. But they know now. They can see all the tiny little cracks like a back of a plate. Fluorescent light . . ."

"So why don't you run a tight ship again?"

"Too late. Anyway, I'm not that way. It's an act. Whatever way I am, I'm not that way. And I'm not the way I am, like right here. Why aren't I the same way? Like now? Like here? Who the hell am I in front of them? Everyday putting on that tough bastard act like Reckelson. Now there's a real sonofabitch in class. And you know, they respect him! Everybody respects him! I had to observe him once. Quiet. You never saw such a quiet class. No backtalk. Respect. I sat there with those kids, and I hated his fucking guts before the hour was over. He scared the hell out of me, and I wasn't even one of his students! Some teacher."

"What about outside of class?"

"I don't know. I don't know. A hard, fast opinion on everything. How can most people be so *sure?* I doubt everything. Including myself. Try to nail him down and he vanishes with a smart-ass smirk. That's his whole way of teaching — power, put-down. He never reads a fucking thing but the same shit he's been teaching for years. He thinks *Silas Marner* is a great novel."

"I never read it."

"Well, you've missed a great novel. And they're spreading rumors about me."

"Who? What rumors?"

"Everybody, kids, teachers, parents. The words out: I can't control a classroom. I'm not sure of myself. I'm too easy one minute, too hard on them the next. Maybe it's not even a case of being sure. It's just how I react to the daily situation in the classroom. I might be in a good mood, really enjoying what I'm teaching. The kids seem interested. Then all of a sudden Judy Hummel, have I told you about Judy Hummel? She'll start passing notes to the guy behind her. A real tease. Then Caine in the back starts reading his *Hot Rod* magazine. All of this bullshit and more is going on, and I think I'm teaching! Well, I'm not. So I get pissed off. I lose control. I start bitching at them, insulting them, pouring on the punishment, homework and more homework. Which someone in the class will welcome with a fart, or a finger. So, they win, you see? They always do. I'm tired, I'm tired, I'm tired."

"Why don't you say something to the dean?"

"There are no deans. Deans are for teachers. To spy on the teachers, that's all they're there for. Just keep bothering the dean with your problems, and you won't be teaching there very long. They spread the word:

You can't handle the kids."

"What's the answer?"

"What's the question?"

Thank you, Gertrude Stein. Oh come off it, Hassock!

"But it's only your first year! Next year will be better."

"You sound like a sports fan."

"So you're going to quit? After one year?"

"Probably."

"And then what? All the training?"

"What training? How to make a bell curve? How to behave in a community? How to make them learn by doing? Addur was right. It was a cow college. I should have majored in milking and become a dairy farmer."

"You've got a degree, a major in English. You're a certified teacher. You may as well use it."

"There's work of all kinds out there — that's the problem. Maybe I'll be a tool and diemaker like the old man wanted me to be. I'll learn a trade. But I hate factories. I hate all the work out there."

"So teach."

"Not for the rest of my life."

"Try to get into a better high school next year. Apply at one of the suburban schools."

"I'm not the type for a suburban school. That's not my territory. I'm a neighborhood Huck Finn. There is something about me which is stamped: lower class. In suburbia they would stuff me in the basement with the janitors. Anyway, I don't have a Master's, the ticket to a better way through education in the suburbs. Do you really think it's any better there?"

"Better kids."

"Maybe. If that's the real problem. Let's go somewhere."

"Where?"

"Just go. Travel. Anywhere."

"Where would we get the money?"

"We've got the money. We're both working."

"You mean spend the whole bank account while you decide what you want to do?"

"Let's go to Europe. Maybe I can teach there when we run out of money."

"We can't waste that kind of money. Not now. What will my parents say?"

"We just go. We explain it to them when we get there."

"You're really crazy. It must be all the wine. It's got to you."

"Let's get out of here."

Hassock, how could you afford to leave that woman? She sounds so sensible.

"Quiet! The bell has rung! Pass in your homework assignments."

"Mr. B., my mother was sick last night so I couldn't do any homework."

"Yes, well you just take care of that old lady of yours. She's more important."

"I hurt my hand in gym, Mr. B. I can't write."

"That should help."

"Hey, Mr. B. I did the wrong pages. And then I lost them . . ."

"What do you mean 'Hey'? Go to the dean's office."

"I did the wrong ones too, Mr. B."

"Tough. The one or two of you who did the assignment, pass it in. The rest of you can go blow smoke out of your ears. I'm tired of your phony excuses."

"What are we supposed to do now, Mr. B.?"

"I'll give you a foreign word: 'study'."

Groans, yawns, loose leaf binders clicking. "Tomorrow's assignment is on the front board. There could be a quiz." Groans, yawns, loose leaf binders clicking.

Only 2:20 in the afternoon of the last class of the day. Another 35 minutes to go. With my attache case opened in front of me, I glanced around the room occasionally to be sure everyone was either working or sleeping.

Linda Lang's legs flashed in front of me, her face buried in a paperback, *Cycle Shack-Up,* her mouth going in circles with a wad of gum. Linda, another punch board, according to Schauk. Most of the guys in class grabbing at her when they though I wasn't looking. Squeezing into her when they came through the doorway. Grabbing her ass when she went down the aisle. She'd open her gummy mouth wide, grin, give them a soft punch in the arm, and then sit down and open her paperback. She didn't know a verb from a motercycle, and she would never need to.

She was ready for the street. Too mature for a high school senior. Although she dressed in a hoody fashion — black clothes, beehive hairdo, a huge leather purse with a can of hairspray sticking out — she was well-groomed. Often she wore heels. And sometimes, to really drive the guys out of their heads, a tight leather skirt and black mesh hose. Like today.

Again she flashed her legs. Popped her gum. And flipped a page. Looked up, opened her mouth wide, and continued reading. She didn't give a shit about anyone in class. Independent. Far out of everyone's range. Almost an adult who sort of sits in the class once in a while.

She squirmed, turned, swung the right leg over the left right in front of me, and kept swinging it in a steady rhythm.

She sunk further in her seat, moved her legs higher and higher, and swung them faster and faster.

This sounds like the begining, Hassock.

The tops of her stockings showed, and then the white of her thighs. She angled a little to the left, and a small white garter, embedded in the fleshy bottom of her ass, peeked out and held firmly to the stocking.

You sure this isn't the beginning all over again, Hassock?

I could feel the warm blood rushing to my face. I quickly moved the attache case around, trying to look busy, not sure myself whether I was manuvering for a better glimpse or trying to block the scene entirely. Rubberbands, paper clips, red pencils . . . I was manuevering for a better glimpse.

Is fiction life, Hassock?

Just then she unconsciously swung her legs straight, uncrossed them at the same instant, swung them wide open in front of me (hair! undoubtedly hair, nothing else!) looked up over her book and caught my eye.

Is pornographic writing literature, Hassock?

She smiled, sat straight up, pulled her skirt down and continued reading. But her eyes glanced at me at the top of each new page, while I did everything I could to look purposeful, rummaging through the attache case, pulling out manila folders thick with themes.

I got up to add the quiz notation to the assignment that was already on the blackboard.

I walked around the room a few times, raised the window a notch, opened the door slightly.

Near the end of the hour, I was seated at my desk again trying to correct papers. My eyes continued to wander toward her legs. Quickly I would catch myself, look up at her, and discover she was no longer eyeing me. Once again, in the final seconds of the hour, she crossed her legs, and I could not free myself from the sight of her white thighs. The bell suddenly shattered the quiet. When I regained my proper teaching posture, I noticed that Linda was gone. A number of the guys smiled at me as they walked out the door.

MR. B HAS A HARDON OVER LINDA LANG!
FOR A FUCKING GOOD TIME, CALL

DU6 2278

(ask for Linda)

Linda
Sucks

Diagram this sentence: Fuck me Linda.

Blackboard greetings before my 1st hour class the next morning.

It hit as fast as a slap or a sudden scream. Those dirty bastards, was all I could say to myself, erasing the board with determined wipes of a wet cloth.

I should have been able to laugh it all off as typically teenager. Something I might have pulled off myself years ago. But I couldn't. It hurt. What's more, I was afraid. They definitely had the edge on me now. This would spread through the school. I would be fired. Guilt by suspicion.

How many other teachers did this happen to? Did Reckelson ever find FUCK YOU on his blackboard in the morning? Would he confess if he did? And Schauk? What about him?

I had to ask Schauk about all this. I had to concentrate on what I would be teaching 1st hour. What the hell was it? Branding. The essay on branding. Read the essay and answer some questions. Maybe we could kill the hour in discussion. Or maybe move through it quickly and save plenty of time for them to get started on tomorrow's assignment. Which gives me time to plan the rest of the day. Those lousy bastards. It's all over the school by now. Branding. What the hell page was that on? I should read it. Skim it . . . just go over the topic sentences. Maybe give them a quiz right off the bat, which will give me time to go over the whole thing myself. Branding . . . what the fuck! Is this American literature? The bell! Christ. . . .

The kids moped their way into the classroom. The second bell rang. In walks Hopgood,the chairman of the department.

"Mind if I sit in this hour?," he said. "I'd like to observe."

"No. Yes. Ah, there's an empty desk in that third row there."

"What will you be teaching today?"

"What?"

"What was the assignment for today?"

"Branding. We're doing branding. Discussing the essay. Here, in the *Adventures in American Literature* text. This page."

"Fine. Thank you. I'll just take that seat then. Pretend I'm not here."

He's not here. Hopgood's not here. He's sitting there bigger than shit, but he's not here. The kids are pointing to him. They know he's here. They know I know he's here. And why he's here. And they are going to fuck me over good, I know it. He's taking out a spiral notebook. I haven't even begun. He's already making notes.

No lesson plan. If he asks to see a lesson plan, I'm screwed. Branding. Give them a quiz first.

"Okay, quiet everybody. The bell has rung. Today you were supposed to read the essay on branding. Close your books now and take out a piece of paper. Just a short quiz."

Groans, moans, books slapping on the desk. "Oh no, not a quiz again?" "Did you read it?" "Did you read it?" "Did you?" "No." "No," chuckle. "Are you kidding?" "Mr. B., I lost my book so I couldn't read it last night." "I read the wrong assignment, Mr. B."

"Quiet!" What am I going to ask them? Stall, stall. How's Hapgood doing? Stall, stall. "Okay, please carefully copy each question as I give it. Leave enough space between questions, and when I'm through dictating them, you can go back and answer the questions in the blank spaces."

"I don't understand?" "We never did it this way before?" "What did he say? What was the question?" "He didn't give no questions yet, you dope."

"Did everybody hear me?"

"No. What was the question?"

"I didn't ask any questions yet. I'm merely giving directions."

"What's 'merely' mean?" Laughter.

"Okay, number one: Who is the author of this essay?"

Moans, groans, snickers . . . a whisper. "Do you know?" Shoulders shrugging, heads turning . . .

"Okay, Cass, close your book." Laughter. Very funny, Cass, you sonofabitch.

"Number two: What kind of essay is this?"

"You mean what's it about?"

"No, I mean what type of essay is this. Remember, we talked about the various types of essays. What type is this one?"

"Rotten."

You bastards. You're really working me over. Every question brought a smart-ass comment. Finally I got to number five where I could turn them loose for at least 10 minutes, and figure out where I was going for the rest of the hour.

Hapgood came up to the desk. "Do you have your lesson plan handy?"

"You know, I'm looking for it myself right now. I'll bet I left it on the kitchen table at home. I was working on it during breakfast. It must still be on the table."

He went back to his seat, writing in his spiral notebook on the way. I borrowed a textbook from a student in front of me and took it back to him with the page opened to the assignment.

"Thank you," he said, pleased with my considerateness.

"Okay, pass in your papers. I'll go over them tonight and return them to you tomorrow."

"Yeah, that'll be the day." "Sure thing, Teach." "What about the quizzes we took the last few days?"

"I've been very busy planning this unit. I'm a little behind in my paperwork. I promise I'll have everything back to you tomorrow or the next day for sure."

"Mr. B., can I go to the john?"

"No. You know better than to ask that. We're in the middle of a class right now. Okay, open your *Adventures in American Literature,* all of you, to today's assignment. And take out the questions you answered for today." Hardly any homework papers, goddam them! Less than half the class prepared to discuss the essay.

The entire discussion was a disaster. Thirty minutes of "What was the question?" punctuated with "I don't know," "I didn't read it," and an occasional "The sun is in my eyes, Mr. B."

In desperation I read them whole sections of the essay aloud. I explained how important branding was, and commented how interesting the various brands were, and what they stood for. I stretched branding to the breaking point of boredom, boring even myself, then gave them an assignment for the next day — a book review: "Triumph in the Arena," based on the novel, *The Brave Bulls.*

There were still twenty minutes left till the end of the hour. Hapgood knew I had failed. He knew damn well that any teacher worth a damn could continue to beat a subject to death for a full period. I was just tired of listening to myself. Bored with branding. Bored with the kids. There were 55 minutes to the hour. You were paid to teach for the full period. And here I was, short-changing the system. Ducking from my responsibilities. Hapgood, I wanted to tell him, Hapgood, you caught me empty-handed. Just plan empty. Hapgood, I'm no fucking teacher.

I started correcting quizzes. Hapgood was still writing in his spiral notebook. When the bell rang, he got up with the rest of the students, smiled, pretended he was in a hurry, and handed me the notes as he ripped them out of the spiral.

"Hey, I heard Linda has the hots for him," I heard in the hallway, as I'm sure Hapgood heard, but neither of us admitting it.

"Look these over," he said. "We'll have a conference sometime tomorrow and go over the details then. Thank you for letting me sit in."

"Okay. Thanks for coming."

The notes were hastily written but well organized into three parts: personal, techniques, assignments.

PERSONAL

"Okay, okay, okay, okay" Watch! Weak crutch.
Covering your mouth with your hand — work on enunciation.
Terrible enunciation for an English teacher (Foreign background?)
Restless walking.
Relax with class. More give and take, more freedom would keep the working atmosphere.
Well groomed.
Look at the kids individually, not as a class. You have a tendency to talk at them (at anything) whether the audience is responsive or not. (Do you believe in what you say?)
Watch that students are not working in other subjects during work period for English (during all of English) . . . a girl doing shorthand, a boy reading an automotive magazine, another girl reading a letter, a boy with his head on the desk sleeping, at least five students without textbooks (how many did the assignment?) one girl reading a scurrilous paperback bracelets jangling on some of the girls. Very distracting.

TECHNIQUES

Insist that homework assignments be done. (Why were so many people unprepared?)
Demand that students keep their voices up.
What are you doing to pull the slower ones into the act?
Any personal experiences in the class? How many have been on ranches? What is our West like? How many have seen movies about the West? (Too much teaching from the book.)
Branding—tying this in with cars is a good technique. Aren't our cars branded? (Perhaps this would bring in the boy reading the automotive magazine.)
Other examples? Boys brand girls. "Brand" names. What about working at some brands for members of the class. Might be good incentive for checking derivations of names.
Other forms of branding? (relation to cruelty?)

Humans—tatooing
piercing of ears
Animal—docking tails
clipping ears

ASSIGNMENTS

Be sure that everyone is listening. (One girl was reading a letter.)
Another group of girls was passing around what looked like an obscene book, *Cycle Shack-Up*.
Perhaps they need more help in knowing what to look for regarding the assignment. Example: Since they have probably all heard about bullfights, you might have used that to your advantage in introducing tomorrow's assignment. Foreshadow the excitement for them.
Chairs in a circle for discussion—a possibility.
Use of blackboard—fair. Not enough time for them to grasp anything. You erase too quickly. (Very difficult to read your handwriting. Print.)
Make the girls in the front row sit up straight. (Too distracting for the teacher.)

H. Hapgood.

I dreaded the thought of the 6th house class. The morning message on the blackboard haunted me all day. How to face them? How to avoid facing Linda? This is what teaching had become: offense vs defense. Time wasted in searching out the other's weak spots and then pouncing on them. Nothing left now but to go through the motions with them till the end of the school year. Keep order. Try not to be fired. Maybe bend a little, if they would let me.

"Okay, the bell has rung. Will you people please sit down?"

"Hey, Mr. B., somebody told me you like to drink a little."

Cass again. I should have cut him down, really stomped him into the floor; but for the first time, I smiled a little, almost laughed out loud. A hell of a way to begin a class. And only he would come out of left field with such a remark.

"No, Ed. Never on the job," I answered and broke up the class. Common ground. For the first time we were all laughing together.

"Okay, let's hold it down. Let's, let's just talk for a while." I got up from my chair, sat on the edge of my desk and began to confront them as honestly as I could. I went out there, right in the open, feet dangling to the floor, cool as could be, and tried talking with them.

"I want to talk seriously with you for a moment."

"You got exactly one minute, Teach," a voice shot out, followed by a ripple of laughter.

Again, I laughed too. "Thank you. I'll try to stay within that time limit. We're getting near the end of the year, and there are many things I would like to say to you people, to this 6th hour class in particular. You have not been easy for me, and Jesus, I've tried."

"Are we all going to pass?"

"That's not the question. What's important is whether or not you deserve to pass. Whether or not you think you've done your best."

"For what?"

"Well, for yourself. For everybody else. For your parents, you, your future. All that. When June comes along you're going out in that cold world. A job, most likely. Maybe a little more school for some of you ("Boo, boo, boo!") Cut it out! See, that's what I mean. Immaturity. You hate school now only because you don't understand how important it is. How much it will matter years from now when you're saddled with all sorts of responsibilities — wife, kids, house. There just won't be enough time to get a better education. There won't."

"Who needs it?" says Ed Cass. "I'm going to work for my old man at the gas station. I don't need no grammar, no branding, none of this stuff."

"You'll see, Ed. Every student in America probably asked his teacher the same question at one time or another. I felt that way myself once. It's a game. Just one of the many games between student and teacher. Christ, it must go back to Colonial times. Make the teacher look like a fool. Say things behind his back. Spread rumors. Fill blackboards with profanity, like somebody did this morning on mine."

"What's profanity?"

"Just another form of language. Let's not get off the track. I'm talking about something entirely different. I'm talking about respect for people. Not just me, but everyone you come in contact with, especially those who seem different from you. I'm talking about respect for teachers. You just don't sneak into a classroom and write FUCK YOU on the blackboard and expect a teacher to love and understand you!"

The words cracked into the air and shocked everyone, including me. I had no intention of voicing them in class. Yet, there they were. And the class would neve forget them. I was on my way to becoming 'legend' at East Campbell High. Everything that followed was spoken in an air of mutual embarrassment. I began tripping over my own words till I finally lost whatever else I had intended to say, wondering how the hell to end it all.

"You see, I'm not here for my health. I'm certainly not in this goddam classroom for the money. Can't you at least respect a teacher for what he or she has sacrificed for you?"

"My old man says you teachers got it made." Cass again. "He says he'd like to work your hours ever day and have a three month vacation instead of bustin' his ass the way he does."

"Yeah, that's what my old man says too." "Teachers got it made." "Any dumbbell can teach, my Ma says."

"Okay, okay. I'm not talking about work or money or smarts or anything like that. I would like to think that someday, if I'm any good at this at all, I would be happy to teach for no money whatsoever. Nothing!"

"Then you are nuts," a voice from the back of the room.

"Who's the idiot that made that crack?"

"You got no right to call us idiots."

"I've got every right in the world to call you what I think you are. And when you act like this, completely oblivious to what I'm trying to tell you, you're all a bunch of damn idiots to me! You don't want a teacher. You want a cop like Reckelson. Or some old maid you can crap all over. Well, I don't want to be either one. I give up. You can sit here on your dead-asses for the rest of the year for all I care. You can write FUCK YOU on my blackboard every day. I don't give a shit. I don't owe you anything!"

An undercurrent of whisperings began. I made no effort to stop them. I merely continued raising my voice.

"Homework is going to continue. And it damn well better be done or you can kiss your diplomas goodbye. It's no skin off my ass if you don't graduate. And I intend to find out who wrote all that stuff on the blackboard, and when I do, that person can just forget about graduation this year."

The door opened, and a head popped in: "Mr. Blazen, would you step out here a minute, please?" Whittle, the superintendent, was standing in the doorway.

"Excuse me, class. Please open your books to today's lesson and review."

"What lesson?"

I moved anxiously to the doorway, nodding a hello to the superintendent, and stood stradling the entrance, keeping an eye on the class.

"Close the door," he said. "Mr. Blazen, what is going on in that room?"

"What's wrong?"

"I've been standing outside your door for over 15 minutes. I'm shocked, Mr. Blazen. Shocked! This is chaos. I don't know how else to describe it."

"It's a bad class. I can't help it."

"You mean it's been like this all year? I've heard runors you were having difficulties executing class discipline, but never, never did I expect all this to be going on."

"They won't listen. They won't do anything I tell them."

"Why don't you try teaching instead of lecturing them, baby-sitting them?"

"I didn't go into teaching expecting to be hired as a babysitter, Mr. Whittle. I don't know why I went into it."

"You seem very confused, young man. Out of order, to say the least. I will speak to Mr. Hapgood about this performance. Perhaps we should bring it up before the school board as well before contracts are renewed."

"I'm sorry."

"You know, Mr. Blazen, I shouldn't say this, but I get more phone calls about you than anyone else on the staff. You have made a lot of enemies. Parents do not enjoy having their children ridiculed in class. It doesn't take much of a teacher to call a child an idiot. You don't tell a disadvantaged youngster, as you did, Mr. Blazen, to quit school and join the Army while the recruiter's still in town. That's not teaching, Mr. Blazen. And neither is any of this business I've been listening to outside your classroom."

"Guys like him don't deserve an education. They're not ready for it."

"But they're ready for the Army, are they, Mr. Blazen?"

"Give me a class of good kids. Give me some kids who want to learn. I'll show you what good teaching is."

"Don't be absurd, Mr. Blazen. A good teacher welcomes a challenge. A good teacher is one who can control his class, teach everyone despite personal prejudices or whatever obstacles. Look . . . look what someone put on the blackboard:

MR. B IS A PRICK

Is that respect? Is that control? That just doesn't happen in other classes where conscientious teaching is evident."

"Excuse me," I left him at the door and returned to the classroom. "I asked you people to be quiet. That's the least you can do since you've obviously finished studying. And just plan to remain in this class till tomorrow, if I don't find out who put this on the blackboard. Linda, erase it please."

Linda got up, pulled her skirt down, and was immediately greeted with whistling and sucking noises. She smiled, swung her ass back and forth as she walked to the board, and stretched her rear end to full view as she wiped the words away. Sucking sounds gave way to sexual ummph's.

"That will be enough. Just enough!" Whittle came storming through the door. "Young lady, sit down and mind your decorum. Sit up straight in that chair. Show some decency, please. Now young man, you, give me your textbook, please. What was today's assignment? Mr. Blazen, what page, please?"

"I don't know."

I sat at my desk, staring into my attache case while Whittle wowed them for the rest of the hour, fawning over them, cracking stale little jokes which they found hilarious, winning their confidence. Five minutes before the end of the hour, he slyly walked back to Cass' desk and confiscated a note that had been passing around. He glanced at it, then tossed it into my attache cass just as the bell rang and he and the class departed.

> I know a guy his name is B
> he's a bastard, you can see
> He likes cigars real blunt
> He sticks them up Linda's cunt
> Here and there a little he'll linger
> but look out ass here comes the finger
> who went and done this naught caper
> who went and stold his toilet paper.
> Of arts he is a reader, that is
> if he's not plain with his peter.

I closed my attache case, locked it, and headed for home.

Somewhere between Campbell City and Chicago I began laughing and talking to myself. Imagine Whittle getting his hands on that note! He deserved it, the sonofabitch. That poem ... great poem. Where the hell did I put it? Did Cass come up with that? Naw, Cass ain't that smart. Maybe, though. Maybe. Fucking Whittle ... wonderful wonderful. Good ole Cass. Or whoever.

Tell us about that other poem, Hassock. That "found" poem you overheard in the halls of the last school you ever taught in. The one you put on the blackboard as Poem of the Day:

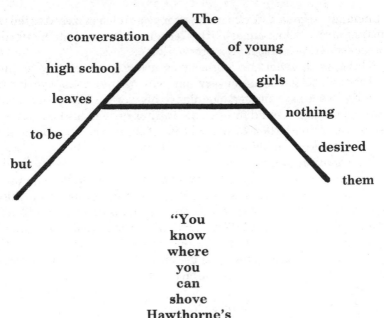

The
conversation
of young
high school
girls
leaves
nothing
to be
desired
but
them

"You
know
where
you
can
shove
Hawthorne's
Scarlet
A
don't
you?"

Reckelson was a teacher. A sonofabitch, hated, feared — but a teacher. And Hapgood was a teacher. Probably the finest I ever saw working a classroom. In the first five minutes of my visit to his class, I could sense he was an artist. He joked with them; he carefully guided them through everything he expected them to see. He sparred with them, creating false openings and then deftly laid in the winning punch. His kids were maybe a little better than mine, but he mixed it well. He did boring things too, old fashioned things like constantly reviewing what a good sentence was. Teaching by repetition. Yet everytime he reviewed a point with them, he carried them still another step further. I never saw anyone teach like that before. He was a master teacher.

But it must take years and years of doing the same thing over again to achieve this. And was it *really* teaching? He never had to glance at the book. He knew everything. Is that what I'm supposed to achieve after 20 years of teaching the same thing? Is that what the kids need? An old man, a veteran of the blackboard they can trust? Imagine teaching the same fucking books, the same goddam literature, *Silas Marner* for crissake, and puking up the same feeling year after year. What makes a teacher like that keep from killing himself? Or Reckelson? What made him go? Go where? Running in place . . . masterfully.

Schauk was something different. Should I be another Schauk? Another lifer sitting around every day reliving the past. A patriarch of sorts. Everyone listening and laughing to his stories. Both young and old listeners. He had wanted to become a writer once in his life. And now, instead, he wrote letters to the editors of *Time,* the *Atlantic,* and the *Saturday Review.* An old rebel. Snuffed out.

What happens to the old rebels, Hassock? What happens to the fire?

Is the past enough? Do they take comfort in the safety of tenure? Is that the way to be? Even receiving a little acknowledgement from the administration: "Oh, yes. We have true individuals on our staff like Ted Schauk. A great old guy, still full of hell at times. There aren't many Schauks left. We'll miss Ted when he retires."

I thought Schauk might just be my man. He came into the classroom like a poet. Always books under his arm. Thick gray hair and a big brush of a mustache. Blue eyes secretly at play. A baggy corduroy jacket, colored shirt, and always a plaid bow tie.

He faced the students almost expecting to be made fun of, laughed at . . . laughing at himself. "Well, look at me. Ain't I the craziest sonofabitch you've seen all day? Is there anybody else like me at Campbell High? Am I an original, or am I an original?"

His teaching was neither technically perfect like Hapgood's nor dictatorial like Reckelson's. And certainly not straight from the book and insecure like mine. It was stylish. Class. A mixture of everything I had seen or experienced. He could switch spontaneously from a lecture to a discussion, from questions and answers to lively explanations heavily steeped in storytelling. When everything was really going well, kids and teacher meshing perfectly, he seemingly taught them nothing, just asked the right questions. The great beauty of his class was the unexpected.

The kids came in with assignments completed, with respect for him, and with a little uneasiness because they were never sure what might happen since Schauk taught according to how he felt. He was a free man, about to retire. In the absence of fear, he enjoyed himself and expected his kids to do likewise.

"Today," he'd say, "I feel like reading out loud. And you're going to listen. I'm a very good reader, you know that. Listen to this. I'll read slowly so that no one misses anything. And if I do come across a word you are not familiar with, raise your hand so I can explain it to you. That way you may learn something about vocabulary. Prefixes and suffixes. The root meaning of words. Some people say that the extent of your vocabulary is in direct proportion to the amount of money you will make in your chosen profession. I never learned more than 250 words. So you see what happened to me.

"Now what I'm going to read today may not interest you in the least. That doesn't matter. It interests me. It interests me and delights me enough to want to share it with you. So listen, and don't ruin this for me.

"The story is called 'University Days,' and it was written by a man named James Thurber. A very fine American writer, American humorist. I don't suppose you ever heard of him before. He's not in your textbook. You know, James Thurber was quite a character . . ."

And so he would go on explaining, remembering, retelling the best of Thurber. He would draw some of Thurber's dogs on the blackboard, some of Thurber's women, and explain why they looked the way they did — much to the delight of the class. Schauk, in a way, became Thurber. And the kids loved Thurber (or Hemingway, Sandburg, Vachel Lindsay, etc.) alive in their classroom. He did the whole Walter Mitty routine — acting out all the parts, the kids screaming. He gave life to almost every thing he taught.

At times he was so overcome with the material he was reading that tears welled in his eyes. Watery-eyed or not, Ted Schauk continued with the story, the poem. And the kids felt everything that was going on inside of him. He was the only teacher they would ever have who could convey what literature meant to the human spirit.

And I wanted to be Ted Schauk.

But of course I could not.

I was called into Whittle's office at the end of the school year and asked to resign.

"If you have to write a recommendation for my records, Mr. Whittle, tell it straight. Don't say I was a good teacher, if I was horseshit. And say I was fired. I didn't resign."

"Good day, Mr. Blazen. I wish you success."

"Just say, 'You're fired'."

"Goodbye."

"Fuck you."

Is that it, Hassock? The End, Part I? Is the story still beginning? Don't rest. Don't fall asleep, Hassock. Sleep is death, remember? Wake up! Are you dreaming of the lions again, old man? Where are the plans to this madness?

Part II

Epitaphium to his death, which read,
The Good Man Has No Shape, as if they knew.
—Wallace Stevens

Hexagram 32

Heng The Long Enduring

```
─────────      ─────────
─────────      ─────────
───────────────────────
───────────────────────
───────────────────────
─────────      ─────────
```

This hexagram symbolizes thun-
der accompanied by wind. The
Superior Man stands so firmly
that he cannot be uprooted.

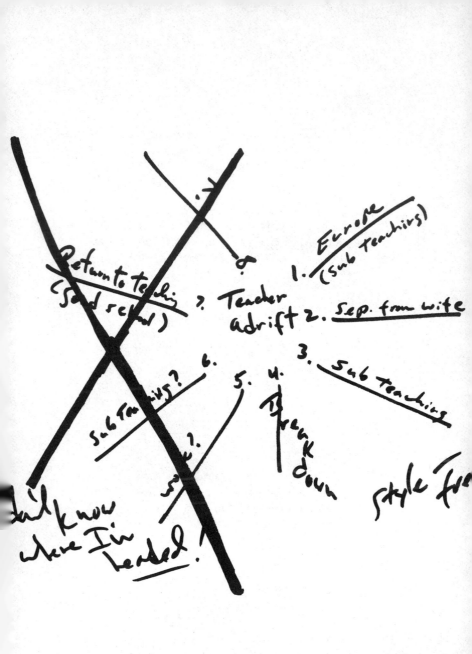

Europe
(Sub Teaching)
1.

Return to teaching
(Send resume)

? Teacher
adrift 2. Sep. from wife

3. Sub Teaching

6. 5. 4.
Sub Teaching? Break
Down

Style Fr

still know
where I'm
headed!

Part II Self-Conflict (creating the life)

Part II . . . break

PATTERNS
> —grad school?
> —Mexico?

SETTING
> —mind?
> —Mexico
> —Europe
> —madhouse?

That was the summer . . . that was summer . . . that was a summer of Mexico then. X marks the story. The beginning end. "The young are the old," said Carlos Merida. Without an X in his name.

The journey then . . . all journeys, *el camino real a muerte.* Where I learned to die. I crossed the border into Nuevo Laredo and discovered what my country had been hiding from me. Nobody dies in America; nobody lives. Nights submit to the electric gods of light. Nights are coddled with cans of beer, silent men and women, the ever-after of television. And death shall have no dominion. It shall have its place, its time, its obituary event. "He shall be waked for three nights at the Klaus Funeral Home. No flowers please. Internment, Holy Cross Cemetery, 3 P.M."

No flowers. Please. They remind the living too much of the dead. Flowers for Mexico. Flowers for the living dead. Death laughs at the border with a mouthful of bougainvillea and says: *"Bueno.* I want to show you something."

And death shall have its dominion. Each step, each mile carrying a 20th Century American into another sun. People baked into the mountains and the earth. Gold of Christianity on their skin, black blood of Indian, Spaniard, coursing in the veins. They lean into shadows on the wall — to love is to kill. He listens to the silence in their eyes.

It takes the timelessness of day and night. Much mountain, moon, star and sun to touch and tempt another shape. Shape of head, shape of limbs, shape of hands, shape of body.

America dropped from my back pocket somewhere back there over the border. I sit on a bus afraid. In the midst of dark heads spouting black words. A bus careening dangerously through mountainous nights, through mariachi music and the rhythm of death on every side.

The women beside me, my wife, American, tightens my hand white. Tries smiling and hiding pictures from back home — just plain Sunday folk worshipping young, Good Man God at the local Baptist church. Mom and Pop and all the fine neighbors of Our Town; Chicago and the busy bus of strangers headed to the daily work of death; stoplights, safety islands, safety warnings; home. Home and the protection of your own automobile. This is my Car. I am the Driver. Step aside, Mr. Death. Who the hell you think is driving this vehicle?

Mr. Death is fat and happy, dressed in blue, flying his own bus over a road somewhere below lit faintly by one headlamp. Held captive by stars and moon and a fiesta of Mexican silence. The woman across the aisle sucks a bright lemon, her child an orange.

Drive on, Mr. Death. The sun and moon are beside me.

The heaviness of sun, of heat. The weight of life and death. The energy of food. Mexican food burning a song to the body. Know your food. Feel it. Know your mouth, your tongue, your gut, your ass. With the sickness comes the scent of soul. Know that sanitary and sanity are one. And one and one equal death. Impurity permits the chance of life.

I drink bad milk, I taste raw fruit, I swallow tamales whole, I chew seeds — whatever the street vendor offers. I thank him for his courage. Compliment him for the artistry of the box hanging from his neck, the box from which he dispenses a dose of death with a smile . . . *gracias.*

Dysentery, altitude/fever . . . 101, 102, 103, 104, 105 . . . I lay in a bed somewhere on a street called Xicotencatl. Xicotencatl, Xicoten, Xico, X . . . I repeat . . . Xicotencatl. It is a sound worth saving, worthy dying with on the lips . . . Xicotencatl . . .

The American wife sits in a bright red and flowered chair somewhere beside me. Waiting. Praying. Distraught over the madness of such a journey. "He is going to die. I will be left here alone. Home is thousands of miles away. This is another country. Where did we come from? How far is America? These silent people of the mountains and jungles. What do they know of modern medicine. What do they care. What do they value in life? Are they aware that modern medicine has diminished the death rate all over the world?"

Send for the Indian doctor. Begin the tribal dance. Let loose the sun god. Start the ancient rhythms of the dances, the chants. The Aztecs. How did the Indian know that men had need of feathers? Doctor! Doctor!

Death! Speak! A man from a land where God shed His grace lies dying. Doctor Death, he has swallowed the sun.

Xicotencatl. Xicotencatl. *El professor,* they call me. Teacher, I say. *El professor de los Estados Unidos. El professor* who tried to teach the young "Triumph in the Arena" and failed because neither he nor the young had ever lived with death. *El professor* on the run. *El professor,* teach me to die. *El professor de los professores.*

The doors of my room are swung open to a patio of night and stars and jasmine. If it must be here, it must be on Xicotencatl with the scent of jasmine. Quixote and Panza are watching. Hand carved wooden figures standing there on the bureau near the door. You make me die laughing, the two of you. You were to come home with me, you madmen. I had a place for you in my room in Chicago. Priests, light a candle before each of them. I can't decide who I love more.

"You are going to be all right. Don't worry. I found a doctor. He said the fever is breaking. He will be back later. Just rest. It was the pork you ate. The pork was cooked improperly. Even the Mexican doctor said Americans must be careful of what they eat here. What a terrible country! So filthy. I'll starve before I eat anything else. I'll live on tea and crackers. In a few days we will be out of here for good. We'll hire a private car, even a plane if we must, anything to take us to the border. You just can't eat everything here, don't you remember? I told you. You don't listen to people. Those Americans I met in town, they even carry their own drinking water. Stay away from fruit and vegetables. Never eat anything from the streets, anything! Eat only in the best hotels. Hurry and get well. Please. I'm not sure I even trust that doctor. He laughed when he took your temperature. How do we even know he's a real doctor? Do you know what his first name is? Jesus."

The beauty of the bullring is death. It is not a question of anything at all. It is a matter of fact. An absolute of a circle, a man, a bull. Illusion helps. The sun for one. The sun at 4 o'clock in the afternoon, cutting the ring in half, *sombra y sol.* The battle cry of the band, horns churning the blood of any man alive to charge — charge anything: another man, a barrera, a windmill, a bull. Always because of the strength that feigns motion.

Chamaxo, *el torero.* Chamaxo, a novillero. Novilleros make bad toreros. Youth takes the wrong chances.

To die a man is to celebrate death. To honor it with flowers, music, and the company of other men and women. The ring's the right place for dying. I don't know where it's likely to go better. You have set your own time by the sun. The *traje de luces* befits the celebration. And there is no need for pockets. Only brilliance to cover the sun.

Your mastery of body movement — be it steps, carriage, the waltz of the arms — will be emulated for days by every man and boy. Inevitably he becomes you and takes that first step with you from behind the barrera. He steps with you all the way through that life and death in the afternoon. Later at the cantina, he talks your talk, drinks your drink, loves your love, dies your death. Only gradually, in the hours and hours of hot sun to follow, does he grow to recognize and remember himself — and live again for Domingo, 28 de junio a las 4 P.M., Plaza de Los Torros.

Xicotencatl. *El professor* lay dying on Xicotencatl. The American professor who is no professor and hardly a teacher. The American professor who was not careful. Too young, lie Chamoxo. No one in America sells death on the streets. In sanitation we trust. In health.

San Luis Potose, Tuxpan, Toluca, Orizaba . . . where does the gringo lay dying? *Calle de Xicotencatl* is all I know. Queretaro, Guadalajara, Popcatepetl, Xochimilco, Paraso, Chichen-Itza, Mexico. *El professor* is aflame. His eyes glow in the dark in a room opened to a patio of jasmine and stars somewhere over the border. On a street that rings with bells . . . Xicotencatl, Xicotencatl, Xicotencatl . . .

Do not eat the fruit. But the open market sings. Who can deny a peasant her costume, when the oranges, the mangoes, fill so fully the brown hands, the black eyes? Fruit made to be touched in the sun. Offerings.

Serapes, huraches, sombreros, leather of umber luster, tamales, tortillas, children washing their hands in sun seeds. Copper and silver. The smell of food, earth, rain, sun, night. Eating an orange, I follow the man with the tiny tiny cages tiered on his back, twice his height. In each wooden cage, soft explosions of bright green. I follow the vendor of baby parrots till I fall.

Xicotencatl.

Fiesta. Lightning in the mouth. Offerings, fire, music, food, women and drink. The Feast of Sante de Christo. Night and a pinwheel of fire stopping too soon in silence. Sometimes, death.

I walk down the streets of stone, with mud houses awash in candlelight and stars. Chili. Tortillas sizzling in oil. A guitar stretching the night of her hair. At the cantina there is this life in us, me and her . . . a clay bowl of pulque.

Later, making a language of ourselves in the fields, neither of us aware of the other's words, we make a love mixed with brown and white hands, hair, burning breath, juice and earth.

Now I am of your color, I say to her.

She rubs the dry earth into my back.

Morning and the cathedral. The cathedral hand-carved by Indians centuries ago. The truth of it all — outside. The inside for manmade Christs. The outside for gods — mazes of stone gone mad with figures, flutes, spirals . . . heads of beasts, of angels, of saints.

Each eye a flame, I open them wider to the night. Quixote. Panza. You bastards, you got me. Mmmm the jasmine. And where is Zapata?

"Do you feel better? The fever's gone down. Try sleeping some more. In a few days we'll be home."

Zapata. No Zapatas for America. No Villas. Their very names sound dangerous. We could never afford such men. Give us mild mannered men to lead us, Oh Lord. Sanitary men. Men of reason and no passion. Our revolutionaries we render comic or comfortable, and we so seldom award them the crown of myth. We build monuments to honor declarations, not men. Tolerance: our virtue and our death, Amen.

The revolutionaries, the people, the artists. They are all the same, are they not, Zapata? They are all one and so many and everyone. No wonder the miles of Mexican murals — there is so much to put down to remember. No miniature art for Rivera, Orozco, Siquerios. Give me the mural to make our life. *"Los Elementos y el Hombre Techico,"* Rivera calls it — his view of the new order. But it was Siqueiros who caught the man, *"Nuestra Imagen Actual,"* the madness, *"El Eco Del Llanto"* — and Orozco who painted it all with fire.

Xicotencatl. The birds. The heat. The tropical shower of green parrots.

That afternoon at the cathedral. The requiem mass. The bells tolling beautifully. The sun so white, so intense, that even the flowers of life and death, the wreaths, the bouquets, had to be turned over on the burning tops of the funeral cars, or tossed in the shade of trees lest the petals turn ashes. Such a sweetness to the sun, the dark Mass being sung, the procession in black about to begin.

In a cantina across the plaza I watch and drink to death. To cut flowers that swallow the sun. To small boys in the market place loosening tarantulas from crates of bananas. Tying strings to their hairy bodies and walking them down the hot streets in the laughter and praise of old men.

To the black bull that stands dazed, sweating wine, pawing the circle of earth, *sombra y sol.* The burden of his body is staggering, yet he stands holds it in place, banderillas deep into his flesh, swaying like batons. Movement to his eye. All his weight will not kneel under as long as movement ahead is perceived . . . and loved to death. And so he moves . . .

77

Xicotencatl, Xicotencatl . . .

"The fever is dying. Here, take some tea."

Chamaxo is dead. He decided the bull was tired and would move unnaturally. And the bull came straight on, *a las cinco de la tarde.* Chamaxo is dead.

I am alive.

The young are the old, said Carlos Merida.

The young . . . I am the young, said Orozco.

After the dying, nothing is the same. *Because I could not stop for death,* I lived to tell about it. To *begin* to tell about it — a fledgling storyteller, Hassock, my mind's name, mostly telling stories to myself. A Chicago novillero, *numero uno* in my own notebooks. *My life had stood, a loaded gun,* so I stalked Chicago's streets, looking for real life, looking for fire, in search of a character I needed to create.

Oh, I could tell you stories you wouldn't believe.

One thing about writers and poets, soldiers and bullfighters, gangsters and old Chicago newspapermen: they celebrate their madness either openly (waving a red flag . . . the whole body, hands, feet, head swinging) or locked inside the head, somewhere between the horns. They're all hellbent for private or public destruction.

Take Lionel O. Inside and outside, every word of his mouth (triggered to the written word of his hand) is a pure invitation to death. He works the keys of the typewriter with both fists. A clean warrior who keeps the action always out in the open. Whether he's writing about War or Peace, for the public or posterity, his only message is: "Line up, gentlemen, one punch to a customer."

Note the honor of the challenge, the dignity of the man: "gentlemen" he calls the big black bulls who wait and the dark end of long Chicago alleys. (There are no rings in Chicago.)

I know all about these things. I have observed many bulls in my day. But with me, it was all locked on the inside. Till I met Lionel O'Roaragan.

Oh, I had read about him, heard about him, talked about him, even tried teaching one of his great poems:

> Go, Ubangi
> Send your murky storm into a
> Night that's wild with the
> Insanity of frothy dogs.
> I'll follow you all the way, Ubangi,
> Into the final madness.

He was where the real challenge was. I knew because I read it all in his weekly literary broadside, *War*. And here I was, or there I was, a neighborhood conscientious objector who thought the world needed saving through model teaching! And damn, there were guerrilla-goings-on, hand-to-hand combat, raids, invasions, landings, sabotage and bombings. All right here in the city. Right on the Chicago front. And O'Roaragan was leading the best damn crack company of poets and novelists and critics any city could muster. They fought alongside him. They threw worded grenades at the establishment. And only he could see the face of the enemy:

"Writers, scattered in unwanted seclusion drift with the younger painters and sculptors toward the Oldtown district where the fight is — the War is with the Successful, the Institutionalized — knowing the enemy as only the sycophant who is called artist and is not, who has defamed the arts through faked popularity and bogus achievement."

He fights on all fronts, O'Roaragan. His constant Chicago Battle is the Battle of the New Renaissance: "Strange, diversified and unpredictable, a RENAISSANCE, a second coming of the artist — the whole artist, be he painter, writer, poet or critic — has happened in Chicago. Due to the traditional ignorance and tolerance of an opulent society, of economically purged minorities desperately clinging to their flagging nationalities, of trite, staid, pre-gimmicked newspapers, of useless causes ending in a forgotten chant dirged in the darkness of anachronistic bughouse square, the artist exists!

Did I rendezvous with O'Roaragan immediately? No. I ran into one of his enemies at the time, one of the new Chicago newspapermen of the old school, Hans Hogan. A good man who extended a caring hand to young Chicago writers. How was I to know he was on O'Roaragan's hit list at the time?

"Do you know this guy, O'Roaragan?" he asked me in one of those seedy newspapermen's hangouts below Wacker Drive in Chicago.

"No, but I read him in *War*. He's against everything."

Hogan laughed. "He is. He's paranoiac. He's got this sinister scowl on is face all the time. I think he's the illegitimate son of Ben Hecht."

I laughed. What else could I do? Defend his honor? I mean, a writer I .adn't even met, but probably would someday?

And I did. Pure accident. I was having my tooth fixed by this rotten dentist in a condemned office on the Near Northside when he says to me, between the hmmmmmmmmmm, bzzzzzzzzzz, "So you want to be a writer, huh?"

"Ouch! Sometimes."

"Then you should meet O'Roaragan in the next office," bizzzzzz, grrrrrr, clop!

"Lionel Ooooooooooooooooooo!?"

"Yeah, the character who publishes *War* . . . here, spit it out."

So I stumbled into *War's* office, bleeding from the mouth.

"A writer! Good, sit down. Wait, I'll get my first aid kit. Brought it back from Spain with me where I was an ambulance driver. Me and the rest of them. We weren't lost at all. Can you write a book review? Of course you can, you're a writer, aren't you? I need book reviews for my next issue of *War. War!* Do you know what that means? The literary lifeblood of this whole rotten city! There are enough cretins in the Chicago establishment, but it's nothing compared to New York. Nothing! They're afraid to publish anything that comes from the gut. See those over there by the wall? Twenty unpublished novels! Why? New York. No guts. The whole Midwet is dung to them. But I'll show those bastards. See this typewriter? Carl Sandburg's. Belonged to Sandburg. Then it was my old man's, another great newspaperman. Now it belongs to me. It's up to me. Up to us. Here's a book to review. Blast it! Crap. I'm older than you, buddy. And I'm writing two novels, editing a commercial mag, publishing *War,* and keeping a family together. And I'm getting tired, do you understand? TIRED! But I won't quit. I won't quit like the rest of them. I always said I'll give myself till 60, and if I haven't published a book by then, I'll do two things: first I'll become an insurance salesman. Then I'll kill myself. Here, you want more crap to review? Stacks and stacks of half-baked New York novels, religious diatribe, fix-it books, cookbooks.. . COOKBOOKS! Do you know about cookbooks? That's all the hell they publish now. Chicago a second city, ha! Nobody knows what the hell's going on here. Nobody knows the wars I've waged. Nobody cares. One sagging sycophantic sage of ambiguity, William Murray, wind-passing in a travel magazine, delivered a high-pitched diatribe about Chicago's literary life. Waxing his stupidity in the putt-putting of a cretin unworthy of indictment in Berlioz's "Evenings With An Orchestra," Murray ignorantly stated, 'The saddest of the city's cultural life is the almost total absence of local publications open to native writing.' Untrue, Boobis Americanus!"

We became fast friends. I loved this guy. Before I met Lionel O'Roaragan, I used to think maybe I could be a writer someday. But O'Roaragan made a man *feel* like a writer instantly.

What else can I tell about him? How many men he killed in the war? Around 20. What war? It doesn't matter. He killed a lot of men and he's got medals to prove it. And wounds. A lot of red badges. I haven't asked for any evidence. I trust him his wounds, his medals, his fantasies.

Should I tell of the delicious nights of drunkenness? Where O'Roaragan roosts in Farewell's Pub? Where he has been known to have pummeled — no, punched! — 10 delicate dilettantes in a row at the bar. How he swaggers in most any night, whispering from the side of his mouth: "There are at least 6 guys in here who would like to kill me." Or the time a piper walked into Farewell's, filled his bag, and wailed "Garry Owen" over and over again, awashed in O'Roaragan's tears?

Or the time he had it out with Algren?

Or the tears, many tears, he's wept for Çonroy, Farrell, and Fitzgerald?

Or the night the three of us, O'Roaragan, Loneson, and Hassock went to a roadhouse on the outskirts of Chi just to hear some old Dixieland played? In O'Roaragan's mythical mind, it was Bix playing — only he's real name was KinKaid and he played clarinet. But O'Roaragan said he heard Bix, and kept downing the beer and VO. And Bix it was. "Gimme a horn," he cried the whole night long. "Gimme a horn!" and in the early hours of morning we moved to KinKaid's house and listened to 78's of Bix and Spike Jones. "Gimme a horn!" continued O'Roaragan.

"Where the hell did you pick this guy up?" said KinKaid as he wheeled around the room with an armful of 78's. "He's great. He even looks like Bix."

"Actually," I explained, "he's the illegitimate son of Ben Hect."

"Gimme a horn!" So Bix's, I mean KinKaid's wife, Honeysuckle, pulled an antique horn off the living room wall and handed it to him: "Here, you crazy sonofabitch. Here's your goddam horn. Now go outside and blow."

And he did. He turned slowly from all the noise on the inside and went out into the dark street of suburbia somewhere and started to play. He blew long, sorrowful, false sounds. He blared and blared recklessly into the night until someone remembered where he was and went outside to save him from whatever suburbia (a world he never knew) had in store for a solo horn writer in the early hours of morning.

"Get the hell inside here," some gray-haired guy opened the door and threatened him. "You'll get killed. The cops'll be here. Who is this guy, anyway?" he glanced back into the living room.

"He's the last of the old breed of great Chicago-Irish writers," I yelled through the open doorway. "The drinkers, the fighters, the madmen. And he must be preserved! Leave him alone. Or he'll kill you."

"Get in here, you jerk!" he hollered again at Lionel O.

"This man doesn't understand literature!" I hollored behind the gray-haired man's back.

But the gray-haired man continued to pester the man with the horn and finally went up to him to take the instrument away.

"Stand back from me, old man, Mr. Death!" said O'Roaragan. "Get away. You're too old to fight. You're going to die!"

"Give me that horn," he reached for it and Lionel O. dropped him with a single punch, still holding the horn.

"You're Death! You're Death!" he jumped around the old man. "Mr. Death, I'll blow you a dirge . . ."

Me and Loneson finally got him inside. He put the horn back on the wall. "I've lost the lip, I've lost the lip," was all he said in the car as we glided down the streets of suburbia without headlights, looking for the way back to Chicago.

What can I say about Loneson? A quiet writer, Midwesterner, who keeps it all brewing on the inside. He writes mysteries without corpses and cops. Mysteries of desolate midwestern minds even he cannot unravel. They're all ended, unsolved.

"You're good writers, the both of you," O'Roaragan told us that same night from the back seat of the car, "but you'll never be great. Just leave the big bulls for me."

And then I wrote:

When you return from a journey, any journey long enough to forget what you left, the setting you return to, your own private setting — your city, your neighborhood, your block, your apartment — everything is at once foreign yet familiar. It has been waiting for you a long time, and you do not recognize it entirely. Your absence has had no effect on the apartment whatsoever. No effect on the way the sun each day has continued to cut through the blinds of the front window at a sharp angle, or the settling of the dust, the footsteps of the tenant above, or the faded petals of a windowbox geranium.

You were gone and now you are back. That's all. Now you will give the whole scene life again with the opening and closing of doors, the raising and lowering of windows, the adjustment of light, the on and off hum of the refrigerator. Filling the ice cube tray again. Running the water from the faucet (the first turn, a loud spit of brown water), buying food, the preparation of meals, the sitting down at the table to eat. It is all a beginning. Home again.

The living wears on. In a week, ten days, what was strange, what was so very foreign and hard to remember or comprehend, is no longer where you find yourself at the moment, but where you have been. And who you were.

In time, back home, you become reacquainted with yourself.

What's a man to do now? Begin again? There was teaching. There was Mexico. There is this habit of witnessing and making notes. There is the work ethic of making a living, supporting a wife, raising a family — the American way. There is unhappiness, restlessness, a tendency to dream one's self other lives.

For me, in that moment after Mexico, teaching became a setting where a man might kill some time — not unlike others who had made a profession of doing this. If there was nothing else for me to do now, and with no qualifications to do anything else, then I would work at it once more, if I could, while I waited the next move. And I would reduce it to a matter-of-fact job, as any other. And damn it, I would survive, passing all the students, not working them too hard, letting them have their own way. I would even kiss-ass the administrators, parents and janitors.

I would teach myself to play ball. Bank the paycheck. And plot a European escape.

Substitute teaching was a way back in. Perfect! Good money. Fast money. No obligations. Almost no responsibilities. No briefcase. No books. Dress, almost, as you like. Nobody knows your name or even cares what you're called. "The Sub." Perfect.

And the most appealing factor of all: You don't have to work if you don't feel like it. Very simple. You just don't answer the phone. And even if you do, it's your decision. Never theirs.

There were days when that goddam phone would ring at 7 in the morning: "I need an English teacher today at Donnable High School. Can you take it?"

"No."

Just like that. Fuck it. I don't feel like teaching today. I feel like reading. I feel like walking around downtown Chicago. Or maybe I don't want to teach that particular class because it's the same one I substitubed for once before, and I know the kids are a pain in the ass.

Sub. Second stringer. That's me, exactly. I go in when the other guy's knocked out. But *only* if I feel like it. No lesson plans. Nothing I've prepared for. I wing it.

"Okay, calm down. I realize you're particularly touched today to hear that your teacher, Miss Waddle, is seriously ill and may die." (Stomping of feet. Whistles. Cat calls.)

"What's your name, Teach?"

"Don't ask."

"What are we gonna do?"

"I don't know. If it's okay with you, and if you can keep a secret, probably very little." (More applause.)

"Quiet. I like quiet. That's all I ask. I don't know what you were assigned for today. I don't care. If you have some books with you, study them. Or pretend. Or sleep. But no snoring."

And that's the way it went. Occasionally I had to knock some heads together. But I felt a new kind of strength in doing this. There was something about the freedom I felt in substitute teaching that made me feel at times that this was what real teaching should be. If I was not myself, I was damn close to discovering what kind of a teacher I might have become.

Back at the apartment, the living went on. And the marriage, at times, grew more and more tense. We had a slight scare that Betty was pregnant (neither of us was really ready for this) but that passed.

But tension was building. It began soon after my departure from Campbell City High. There was an undercurrent of resentment. A man out of work in America is dangerous to everyone including himself. The resentment rarely reached the surface, however. Mexico, too — the fear, the madness, the danger of such a journey — was not forgotten. I had come very close to the edge. And I had dragged her right up to it with me, with little thought of what we had left behind, what was becoming of us, what would be waiting for us upon our return.

Back home — a return to the norm as far as she was concerned. Back home — a death worse than anything Mexico could dish out, I was certain.

"What now?" Letters from her mother in Southern Illinois . . . "What is he doing?" Fear, fear, fear that she may have made a poor choice. And now this talk of Europe? And then what? When does he settle down? How secure is substitute teaching anyway? No pension. No insurance. No hospitalization. How could she explain what her husband did all day? He did nothing. "Well, he's working as a substitute teacher momentarily, thinking of entering a master's program somewhere. He'd like us to visit Europe for a while, but that's just talk . . ."

"Why didn't you sub today?" she threw her purse on the kitchen table and closed the door.

"All they had was an opening in math. I can't teach math."

"Well you could at least sit there. Isn't that what you say you do in English?"

"I know the math teacher. He's too damn organized to suit me. He's one of those guys who leaves lesson plans in great detail. First you correct homework, then explain a new problem, then call the kids up for board work, then give them some review exercises, and so on till the bell rings. On top of that, he bitches to the administration if the sub doesn't follow his directions. Fuck him."

"You should have taken it anyway and explained you weren't a math teacher."

"I can't stand up there and make an ass of myself for $25. Anyway, he was going to be out all week."

"You mean you passed up a $125?"

"Please, don't."

"So what did you do all day?"

"I cleaned the place up."

"That's nice, but I'd rather you worked."

"You married a lazy bastard."

"I know that now. Why didn't you tell me that before?"

"I did. I hardly ever worked as a kid. There were always more exciting things to do."

"Like getting in trouble. You sure don't take after your father."

"What are you, my mother?"

"No. Your wife. Your working wife."

"We're going to get out of here."

"How? With all your money? The $125 you didn't make this week? Or are we going to Mexico to live on nothing, roll around in filth, get sick and possibly die like you almost did. Is that living?"

"I'm not sure yet. But maybe it is."

"You're crazy. You're going to drive me nuts. Just be sure you answer that phone tomorrow and take the work. You've been subbing since school started and here it's almost spring, and I'll bet you haven't made a $1,000. Last week you worked three days. The week before, two days. And this week you haven't worked at all. And you expect me to be happy?"

"Yes."

"You're crazy."

"So is my old lady. The old man is taking her for shock treatments now. It probably runs in the family."

"Well you weren't crazy before I married you!"

"Probably."

June. Bon Voyage, you little bastards. I subbed the last three weeks of school. Five classes of junior English, *Adventures in American Literature* again. Made them memorize Emily Dickinson's "My Life Closed Twice" for a week. Then taught them Whitman's "One-self I Sing" and told them he was queer.

On the last day of school I arrived very early and waited in front of the main office till the secretary appeared. The checks were placed in the teachers' boxes the night before.

"All classes will be dismissed at 10 A.M.," she reminded me. "Mr. Peterson would appreciate it if you would keep them busy until then."

"Sure."

"Since Mrs. Simson won't be here for the end of the year, you'll have to clean out the room and put everything in order, Mr. Blazen."

"I understand."

I still had almost an hour before the kids came. I worked fast emptying the desk, the file cabinets, the shelves. In a half-hour everything was packed in boxes and placed by the main entrance. The first school bus would be arriving soon. There were already a few cars on the teachers' parking lot.

Returning to the room, I took a piece of chalk and wrote on the blackboard:

WAIT QUIETLY IN THIS
ROOM UNTIL 10 O'CLOCK.
THEN GO DOWN TO THE
MAIN OFFICE AND TAKE
YOUR REPORT CARDS
FROM MY BOX.
Your Teacher
PLEASE ERASE!

"The young . . . I am the young."
PLEASE COPY

On my passport it said "Artist." I could think of nothing else to call myself. I was not a teacher. "Professor" had a certain dignity in Mexico and might sound impressive in Spain. But I was not a professor either. "Artist" seemed loose enough to play around with for sometime.

Aboard ship, furrowing through the Atlantic in sun and storm, happiness, sickness, drunkenness. The kid in the black motorcycle jacket had set sail!

The old man bitched about my not working, then gave me a list of friends to visit in Yugoslavia. The old lady, who could no longer understand what was going on, had been put into a state hospital for awhile. The old man signed the papers, and I looked on.

To begin in Sweden. The wife fast asleep in a cheap pension in the old city of Stockholm. Slowly adjusting to my solitary sickness. I stayed apart from her during most of the crossing. Many of the passengers wondering whether we were man and wife at all.

She wonders. Suspects. Suspects what a crazy-quilt my mind has become. Though she seems happy, for me, that we are finally here. You can't go home again until you know why. Only then can you begin to imagine your return.

The leaving came hard. Her mother will not forgive me. "You'll get sick the way you did in Mexico." Meaning the both of us, I guess. For the time being we forget her and acquaint ourselves with ways Scandinavian. My wife seems pleased with this.

Shopping. Coming to know the beautiful things these Scandinavians make. NK — a department store as an art in itself. Not a cheapness anywhere. Solid craftsmanship. The home as an art form.

The very color of their glass, the shape of their furniture, the warmth of their light: the art of homemaking. We feel this, the wife and I. If there is one thing we might bring back to our married life in America, it could be this: a sense of home that speaks beauty, nature, and natural love.

There was a glass pitcher that begged to be held. So blue it seemed blown out of the very Gulf of Bolhnia. I held the wife's hand tight at the sight of it. Afraid we might shatter it with our breath.

Teach me to make a home, I prayed. To shape a love, to invite nature and the gods inside, to spend long, cold nights beside a birch fire.

Often, after good times in the city, we would move into the quiet countryside each day by train or bus or bike. The natural, ancient beauty of Sigtuna, where Vikings once walked! The primeval peace of Orrefoers. Only here, in the birch tree woods of dappled green, only here in a transparent quilt of earth and wind; here only should the delicacy of crystal be blown and love-fashioned by the breath of man.

I think of American Beauty in plastic and neon and concrete, stamping the work "anonymous" to the jerking rhythm of the assemly line. While here, the artist has a name. What he makes is his, and there is no reason for imitations. Furniture, glass, fabric — "Designed by ————" becomes one with the art.

Isolation? Yes, not to be denied. But is the natural purity, form, color of their art the outgrowth of a separate life? What of the space between towns? The density of the woods? Isolation? Isolate? Or unity? Spirit?

I, a foreigner, alone this moment in a city whose very language is lost to me, yet I can speak with the quiet of the harbor at night. Others, sharing this love with me, on benches, sidewalks, stretched out on the grass. Swedes, standing, almost all of them separate. Few of them together. Even lovers stand apart.

After too many nights like this, walking the harbor, wanting to walk it alone, it is hard to remember I have a wife. The condition seems contagious. I want from no one.

A late dinner the next night, my wife and I return to the pension where I leave her to pack, wash her hair, and write a letter home. We say nothing. She no longer asks where I am going. Together we sacrifice conversation to the sounds outside the window — automobiles, trolley cars, bells. The opening of a door. The clicking of a latch. We move on. Together. Apart.

Down to Denmark.

I carried her name with me across the ocean. A little piece of paper gathering lint in the inside pocket of my corduroy jacket. Astrid — I tore her name and phone number from the bottom page of the last letter Addur sent me from New Mexico.

> ". . . and she has a sister, your age, a delicious looking woman named Astrid. Look her up. Give her a jingle when you're in Copenhagen. She'll show you the town — you lucky bastard!"

Introductions have always been a fright for me. It takes so long to develop a friendship. So much fumbling before it is felt a direction can be taken — or denied. What's more, Copenhagen had taken such a hold on us, running like kids from one part of the city to the other. The antique shops, the fish market, the Tuborg brewery, the restaurant, Tokanten. Turning corners filled with surprises of cut flowers. Watching small, beautiful blond children sail their own boats.

We rediscovered the life in each other. Late each night we would fall tired but laughing into our bed in the Mission Hotel on Longangstraede, only to find we could not sleep without first making love. And again partway through the night. And all was fresh and feverish like the beginning of young lovers. For this, for Copenhagen, we quietly gave thanks.

There were no thoughts of home, family, work, money. Not here in Copenhagen. This was the fairytale city where endings, if they came, could only be happy and barely distinguishable from beginnings.

"Tonight, let's go to Tivoli."

"But we were just there last night."

"I don't care. I want to go back. I want to go back every night. I want to live there, ride the Ferris wheel, that fantastic merry-go-round. See the trained flea circus again, and sit by the lagoon and drink Tuborg till the place closes. What do you say, woman? Come on, move your pretty little ass off that bed. Goddamn it, I love it here!"

"I'm beat. Honest, my feet hurt. I just want some sleep. You go."

"Are you sure?"

"Go ahead. I'll be fine. You can gawk at the pretty Danish girls all night, without me tagging along."

And so I kissed her good night. And felt for that tiny piece of paper inside my pocket.

I stood at the entrance to Tivoli, waiting for Astrid, enjoying the incredible natural beauty of the Danish women. They were of all ages, and all of them appeared young. There were married couples who held on to each other like lovers, and young lovers who teased and taunted and seemed always on the brink of just discovering one another. Some girls walked in alone, others in groups. And they all moved toward the gates of Tivoli like dancers.

"You do have patches on your elbows, Miro. I thought you were joking."

"Astrid. Your brother-in-law was wrong. He said you looked like Hans Christian Andersen."

"That man. I've talked to him only on the phone. Tell me about him."

"I don't think I can. I don't understand him myself. I think I may be afraid of him."

"Is he dangerous?"

"Yeah, in a way. But I'm afraid of everything. The hell with him. He's over there somewhere in California selling real estate, and we're here, aren't we? And what now? That's the question. Tell me, why are all the Danish women so beautiful? Why are there more brunettes than blonds?"

"Don't talk like an American."

"I'm trying not to. Didn't I just admit that there were more brunettes than blonds in Denmark? And if I ever get to Holland, I promise to send you a post card without a windmill."

"That's better. Now, come, let me show you my beautiful Tivoli."

"Lead, my Little Mermaid . . . ouch! Don't kick! I could have said Ugly Duckling."

Never had I met a stranger, a woman, so easily. In a way, there was no

89

past in our encounter. In fact, there was no time at all.

"Do you like merry-go-rounds?" she asked.

"Yes."

"I love to ride the merry-go-round. I want the blue horse."

"Blue? Then I'll ride the giraffe beside you and hold onto its long neck for dear life. Giraffe? Did I say giraffe? Is this a merry-go-round or an ark? You make mighty strange merry-go-rounds in Denmark. Animals of all sorts. In America we have only horses."

"Only horses? How sad."

"Gray ones, white ones, black ones, brown ones, occasionally spotted ones. But horses, all. Every damn one of them. And once in a while a bench. A bench mostly for old grownups who feel silly riding on a merry-go-round and get on mostly to keep an eye on their kids — so they don't fall off. Ooooooops! Here we go. The music is the same though. Merry-go-round music is merry-go-round music everywhere. It's universal — like love and death. What are you laughing at?"

"Have you been drinking?"

"A little cognac before you came. Can you tell?"

"You and your universal merry-go-round."

"I wonder if there are merry-go-rounds in Russia? In Siberia? Imagine a merry-go-round of black horses in a field of snow! Or China. A circle of dragons in Shanghai. Or Tibet?"

"Or Chicago?"

"My dear Astrid, Chicago is the merry-go-round of mid-America. Everybody's riding everybody else's horse and nobody even knows it's all turning backwards. Not even the horses. Did I tell you about my friend, Arroyo L., the artist who lives in New Mexico? Or am I getting ahead of my story here? Just call me, Hassock. Anyway, Arroyo, former Chicago Indian-teacher of painted face and long hair, wanders through all of New Mexico in search of his tribe."

"New Mexico?"

"Yes. I've mentioned it someplace before. Or will. Again. It means space. I'd like to take you there sometime. Arroyo L. one day, suffering from sunstroke, decided to build his own merry-go-round. The same one he carried around in his head for sometime. A merry-go-round that grew out of neighborhood carnivals in prairie lots. So he built it out there in the desert. A homemade merry-go-round going round and round in the desert, under mountains, magic sun, and turquoise sky. Nobody on the goddam thing. Nothing but space. Arroyo, out of it all on peyote, watching the landscape turn, waiting for the Navajos to come back, and make something more of it."

"Oh, it sounds beautiful! At Tokanten there's part of a merry-go-round on the ceiling. Just a horse."

"I saw that! I saw it! What is it with merry-go-rounds anyway? Pirandello saw it. So did Rilke. Even Salinger."

"What did Rilke say?"

"Don't remember, except . ... 'Some little profile hardly yet begun, over this blind and breathless game'."

"Tell me more about Arroyo."

"He was of my mind. A teacher. A great teacher. I'll get around to him later."

We went on all kinds of rides that night. Later we watched a puppet show and talked to the man who trained fleas. Near closing time we sat quietly by the lagoon, drinking beer and cognac, watching the colored light beauty of the Tivoli night reflected in water.

"Do you like it?" she asked.

"Yes. All of it. We have nothing like this back home."

"No Tivoli in Chicago?"

"We are men of little imagination in the Midwest."

"What do you mean?"

"I don't know."

"We're not making any sense."

"That can't be bad."

"Look, the fireworks! Did you see that one? Like a big flower in the sky."

"I like that."

"What?"

"What you said about the fireworks. I'll close my eyes. You tell me what they look like to you."

"Orange. All orange. With long rays like the sun."

"Beautiful."

"Oh, this is a pretty one. You really should uncover your eyes. It's all white and spread out over the sky like a mobile."

After Tivoli closed, we walked through Copenhagen like lovers, holding hands, stopping to kiss.

"How old are you?" I asked.

"Oh, I am not old. I should think I will not be old ever."

"No, you will not. And I will die a young man."

"Let's not talk old. Have you been to Nyhaven yet?"

"No."

"Then we must go. Nyhaven is very much Copenhagen. At Nyhaven there is your American jazz."

Nyhaven appeared a beautiful harbor etched in a dark corner of the city. We came upon it through the back streets. Buildings and buildings, and suddenly water, a harbor, ships and the sea. I was not prepared for the storybook picture of it all. Not in the heart of a city. It was like tearing up a block of State Street in Chicago and filling it in with water and tall ships with white masts. In the glow and reflections of light and the moon, I was quite overcome.

"It is sometimes dangerous," she cautioned. "Too many sailors who drink too much at times. From all over the world they come to Nyhaven. We will go over there, in the basement. Cool jazz? Hot jazz?"

We walked down the stairs and entered a loud, smoke-filled bar that looked like any other jazz bar in Chicago. And she was right about the music — definitely American jazz, hot. Sax, drums, piano and bass. Even a black guy on the bass.

"They sound good."

"The Danes love them."

"How the hell did they ever find this place?"

"Everybody comes to Nyhaven."

A crowded table, a few of them her friends, made room for us. Astrid talked and joked with them in Danish while I ordered beer and cognac for us, and cast my eye somewhat nervously about. A man could get killed in this kind of joint. Hell, this was Clark Street, the Near North, South State Street, Chicago.

"Well, what do you think?" she asked.

"Not bad. A little strange. I feel like I've been here before. Trouble."

"Why don't you take your jacket off? My friends were joking with me about those leather elbows of yours."

"Cheap jacket. My only one. It started to wear out in the elbows in Sweden, so I had a tailor sew these patches on. Tell your friends I'm a melancholy artist on a journey who has cradled his head in his hands for years. Tell them the tailor sewed the patches on with silver and gold thread, and they're magic! Beware of the powers of a man with magic elbows!"

"Wonderful! Tell me some more."

"I'm full of stories without beginnings and endings."

"Then they're not stories?"

"Notes along the way."

The makeup of the bar, of Nyhaven, suddenly seemed sinister to me at best. Maybe the cognac was beginning to depress me. Maybe I just wanted out of there. I seemed surrounded by workingmen and sailors, drunks, laughter, jazz, threats, and beautiful women. Each time the music began

92

they seemed startled, taken by surprise.

"Tell me more about Addur," she said.

"He was my best friend in college. He went West, young woman, West — to seek a fortune developing land for his father's interests. He's the new Horatio Alger, if you know what I mean. No? Doesn't matter. He'll make a terrible husband but a good man. He will live his days in a number of disguises, and your sister will never really be certain who he is. As it should be, for the good of both. Addur is probably mad."

"She won't be unhappy then?"

"Yes."

"I'm lost."

"Hmmmmm. So are we all. Do you know who said that?"

"No."

"Hans Christian Andersen. You want to hear the story of my life?"

"Yes."

"You've heard it all. For now."

"Then tell me about the other woman."

"Why does every woman want to hear the story about the other woman?"

"To know what she's like?"

"Is there a difference?"

"If there wasn't, there wouldn't be one."

"Right. She exists. Mostly in the imagination of the man."

"Tell me about teaching. Something funny."

"Teaching?"

"You are a teacher, aren't you?"

"I don't know. It says 'Artist' on my passport. See? But I never painted a picture. I painted a woman once. But never a picture. Yes, a teacher. Well, I am not too good. Especially at the English. It shows, doesn't it?"

"What?"

"My language."

"Your language is beautiful."

"Only when covered with cognac, dope, love, certain additives. I can't always use it this way. My life ambition is to study silence. Learn how to speak it. Sometimes I communicate too much. Like in class. When I have to 'teach'."

"How do you communicate too much?"

"By trying to use the language too perfectly. English major. Textbookese. Telling the kids, 'Please answer the questions on page 23 tomorrow, class, and diagram the first ten sentences on page 24 — if not, I'll crack your fucking skulls'."

"Oh, that's not very nice."

"I'm not very nice, under those conditions. I can't get on with it. All I ever get to teach them is *Adventures in American Literature*. That book will be the end of me yet. I once made two classes paraphrase "I Hear American Singing" for 5 days, then read aloud their paraphrases for the next 2 days, then assigned them work on the questions at the end of the unit for another 2 days, and finally wound up the whole thing with a one-day essay test. And all they ever learned was that Whitman was queer — which was what I told them, in an off-handed sort of way, the very first day."

"That's too bad."

"Tell it to the Good Gray Poet. It's the truth. Who says a teacher must be a nice guy?"

"They are the only ones I remember."

"You're right. But they do tend to lend themselves to much suffering. Like Castrati, who was queer. Too easy . . . they shit all over you."

"You can be nice and be careful too."

"Careful. I'm beginning to communicate too much. Before long we'll begin to understand each other. Then where will we be? More cognac, please. More cigarettes, more music, more more. Here's to American jazz. The only good fucking thing we ever gave to the world!"

"What about the bomb?" someone asked. A voice from the bar. Someone I could not see clearly.

"You give the whole world the good bomb because you love us so much, don't you, American?"

"No. I didn't say that."

"You and your goddam bombs, you stink!"

"Me? Why me? I'm the man without a country. I'm just a merry-go-round man myself."

The group had finished its set, and while the laughter and conversation continued, it was scattered. His voice, in clear English, boomed over the room. He pushed himself away from the bar and moved toward me. A sailor, I thought. Scandinavian or possibly German. I kept one hand on an empty beer bottle as he stepped closer. His hands were empty but clinched.

"American, take your bomb and shove it up your ass!" And he spit in my face.

Astrid jumped in front of him, shouting in Danish. He waved her away and turned back to the bar.

"Come on," I pulled her toward the door. The group began to play again. We could hear the muffled rhythms outside as we walked toward

94

the mouth of Nyhaven.

"Let's stay right here and wait for the sun to come up," I said.

"Come. I live not far from here. The next street. I'll get some bicycles for us. We will ride to Klampenborg."

"Bicycles? In the dark? Where's Klampenborg?"

"North. On the sea. On the way to Elsinor. There is a beautiful beach there."

The road to Elsinor was quiet. We pedaled along in the darkness, the sea at our side. We brought the two bikes closer together at times and held hands and laughed. Ships moved in a calm upon the sea.

"Over there, across, is Sweden," she said.

"Can you see it?"

"Sometimes, when the day is bright and clear."

At Klampenborg we dropped our bikes in the sand, took off our shoes, and walked along the beach. I don't believe we said anything for a long while. The sand was cool and the night sky beginning to lighten.

"I understand Danish women undress right in front of everyone on the beach."

"Yes, but not like that. It is done in a way that there is nothing to see, nothing to be embarrassed about. You Americans. Is nude bad? I'm sorry."

She knelt down on the sand and began to undress, loosening her undergarments first, explaining how she could easily slide into her bathing suit, if she had a bathing suit with her.

"You see? It is very easy, and there is nothing to see. Magic, yes?"

"Yes."

"So we will swim, no?"

"No. I'll freeze."

"You won't. Get out of your things."

I undressed and followed her naked across the sand. The water lapped around my feet, my legs, and slashed my ass with an icy shock as I waded in after her.

"I feel like screaming out loud," I said to her.

"Scream."

"No. It's more exciting to hold everything in. Can't explain it. Is that courage? Maybe that's courage. Or craziness. Tell yourself you don't feel it. You don't hurt. It's frightening, the more I think of it. Submitting the body . . . denying it . . . for a kind of freedom of the mind."

"The sauna is something like that."

"Yah, that's right. Scandinavian torture. Or release."

She came into my arms without my even asking. All perfectly natural, understandable, acceptable. I was heavier, warmer than she. Maybe it was that. I touched her breasts, the smallest I had ever felt on a woman. I held them in my fingers like plums. I reached down and cradled her between her legs. Again, without either of us mentioning it, I found myself being led back to the sand by her hand.

"Is it all right? Is it safe? Is there any danger I might give you a child?"

"No. But that would be all right."

"All right?"

"I would like to make many children someday. Make them and love them. Sew clothes for them, knit sweaters, tell them stories. Take them to Tivoli every night. That's what Tivoli's for."

"Then why aren't you married?"

"Marriage. Oh, I don't know. Because then there is nothing else, it seems. I had one child. I lost him. But I don't want to talk about that. You have no children?"

"No."

"How can you be married and your wife happy without any children?"

"I don't want to talk about marriage or children."

"The child's world is a good world and should be ours."

"And what do you do when the child finds out the world isn't what Hans Christian Andersen said it was? You know, that character back there in Nyhaven with his bombs and all that bullshit? He's right. Then what?"

"Then I take the world with me. Like that! And it's all over."

"You make it sound so inviting. When the time comes for me to buy that ending, maybe I'll come back to your fairyland. We'll look for the happy ending together — bicycling to Elsinor, or jumping off the merry-go-round at Tivoli."

"I will soon get a headache talking like this. Make love to me, Miro Magician. To hell with your bombs! Here, sptuu! I spit on your lips. I rub your magic elbows. Make us some sun!"

Something happened to me in Yugoslavia.

We came there, my wife and I, after a long journey by train through Germany, Austria, and Italy. I first sensed it in Trieste, in early winter where the buildings in the main square were cold and gray and sent me immediately into a state of depression.

There was a cafe overlooking the square and the sea that was glassed-in for winter. And inside there was the amber warmth of light and the sting of black, bitter coffee. We waited for a bus that would take us across the border into Yugoslavia. The port of Rijeka was our destination. There we were to find a ship that would take us down the Dalmatian coast to Dubrovnik. And from there, somehow, we would get to Greece.

We had violent arguments soon after Denmark — once it became clear that our money was not holding out, that I was not being as careful with it as I should. We had already wired her parents from Munich for an additional $500. But even with this, for my wife, the journey was over and it was time to return home and get back to work.

Work. There it was again. My work, I felt, was what we were doing, but I could not explain this to her because I did not understand it myself.

"Why don't we go straight to Greece," she said, "spend the money we have left and then fly home? Why waste time and money in Yugoslavia, an Iron Curtain country, where we probably shouldn't be in the first place? I'm afraid of it."

"Don't worry about it. We have visas. We won't spend much there because of the good rate of exchange. I think you'll even like it. The old man was there. He worked somewhere around Ljubljana. He came from Hungary when he was a young man, met the old lady somewhere in Serbia. I'd like to look around."

"What if we don't get out of there?"

"Crissake, don't keep thinking about such crap. What the hell are they going to do to us? I'm sure there are other Americans there. They're not going to lock us up just because we're American tourists!"

"How much of the $500 is left?"

"Enough!"

"We have to pay all this back, you know. And build up the bank account when we get back. We won't have anything. You're going to have to find a teaching job again."

"For crissake, will you please enjoy yourself! I've heard all that before. Fuck the money."

"Sure, 'fuck the money' just like that."

"Oh, go to hell."

We were the only passengers on the bus that left Trieste and began climbing the mountains toward Yugoslavia. At the border, a guard, wearing a red star on his cap, went through all of our luggage and told the bus driver (who spoke some English) to tell me to write on a card he handed me exactly how much money I was bringing into the country and how long I intended to stay.

I jotted down some figures for him, which I was sure made no sense, and before leaving he asked me to remove the navy blue nylon raincoat I was wearing, which I had bought in Rome. He showed the coat to the

Italian driver and said something. The driver nodded. And then the guard returned the coat to me, returned our passports and visas, and left.

As the bus began to move beyond the border station, the driver turned toward me and laughed, explaining how so many of these raincoats were being smuggled into Yugoslavia from Italy, and how the guards could not seem to stop it. It is funny, he said, if you go to Belgrade you will see everybody there is wearing these blue nylon raincoats made in Italy, and nobody knows how they get there. The guard wanted a raincoat too.

Rijeka and the rain. A dreariness heightened by a fear that we were heading deeper into a country that just might consume us. Getting off a bus near the port, unable to find anyone who spoke English, anyone who could help us. The little I knew of their language was almost useless. Finally a small boy led us to a hotel a few streets away from the port.

The next day, after wandering a morning through a city almost entirely without cars, only dirt streets, horse wagons, ox carts, women in black babuskas watching our every move, I found the transport office where we booked passage on a small steamer that left that afternoon down the Dalmatian coast. The wife, by then, was in tears.

I began to grow a mustache in that time — in fact, soon after Denmark. By the time we reached Yugoslavia, the mustache was quite full and I found myself easily passing as one of their countrymen. There was a striking resemblance between me and most of the Yugoslavian men. Only my wife and my American shoes made them wonder. In Rijeka, five or six people approached me alone, rattling away in Croation, shoving fists of dinars in my face. They wanted to buy my raincoat.

Aboard ship, I never removed it. For two days and three nights I was unable to sleep. Since I could not make arrangements for a private cabin, I was given a bunk in a cabin with five other men. My wife was placed in another with two women and three children. The women argued through much of the night, threatening the children, hitting them on occasion. My wife lay awake in fear. I finally paid a steward $10 for a small, private cabin near the engine room. My wife felt somewhat relieved. But even so, I still could not sleep. Then I met Spira, the lawyer.

I was looking for the head our second afternoon out. I pushed open a rusty door on the main deck, and there stood a well-dressed man, wearing a raincoat like mine, smoking and pissing on the floor. He tried speaking to me in a number of languages and finally resorted to a little English. The ship's plumbing was not working, he spoke and gestured. It never worked. It was an old boat, sunk at least three times during World War II.

With each surge of the ship, water and urine mixed on the floor. A single toilet bowl, loaded with shit, ran over and around our shoes. The man, who introduced himself as Spira, a lawyer, explained how I should hold my breath while he lit a cigarette for me. The ship plunged, and the shit flowed over both our shoes.

Spira laughed then crouched and showed me just where and how I might take a crap if I needed to. I nodded no and walked back to the door on my toes. On deck he led me to a faucet where we let clean water run over our shoes.

That night, Spira, my wife and I ate dinner together. Relying a great deal upon gestures, we laughed, ate, and drank, and made ourselves known. My wife, I sensed, was afraid of him.

It appeared no one else could afford to eat from the ship's menu. Most of the people carried fruit and bits of food in cloth bags. Spira, too, had his own food, but he ordered soup for himself and wine for the table.

Later that night, my wife safely asleep in the cabin, Spira and I talked out on deck. The sky had cleared a day out of Rijeka. Stars shone above us and all along the mountain crest that paralleled the Dalmation coast.

It would be more warm now, he explained. Rijeka, no good. Cold like Germany, like Trieste. Dalmatia, ah you see, moon? And tomorrow, sun. Much sun. Trees, plants, everything green. Oranges, lemons. Dalmatia, beautiful. And Dubrovnik.

He was returning from a trial in Rijeka, he tried his best to explain to me. Young man kill fellow worker. I do nothing for him. Can do nothing. He will be killed. Young people problem here, like in America. But no long, no big problem. Just starting. Just starting now young people leave home, leave family for city. Trouble in big cities like Belgrade. Will take long time to change, be different.

The more we attempted to understand each other, the easier it became. He seemed to anticipate my questions, understand the answers I sought. He spoke of the early history of his country. He described the Bogomils, the tombstones they left and what great works of art they were. On a piece of paper he copied Dragats' epitaph for me to keep. I thought, perhaps, someday it could be mine.

"We are a history of blood," Spira said. "From the beginning, blood. The Turks know only blood. And we are the same." He talked of the blinding of 20,000 prisoners in the Byzantine Empire and how they were sent back with only one eye. And the basket of oysters a brave woman carried . . . a basket of eyes torn out of the enemy.

"Once was a Montenegrin," he said. "A great butcher who caught a Turk and with the axe, swoosh, perfectly so body would not be spoiled. Then hacked into Turk's chest and tore out beating heart and throw to a dog. But even dog would not eat heart of a Turk!" he laughed.

"And the Bogomils?" I asked. "Tell me about them."

"Like children. Artists from the beginning. Only joy, nothing else. Look Dragats' epitaph. What mean that?" I shrugged my shoulders and listened to the ship's engine pounding away into the night.

We were to dock at Split at 5 o'clock that same morning. He invited me and my wife to come with him, have breakfast on shore, and see some of the city. He assured me that the ship would be in port for almost two hours before leaving for Hvar and Dubrovnik. We talked through the night.

When dawn broke, I went to the cabin to wake my wife; but she was sleeping so soundly, I left a note for her explaining where I was, then locked her in the cabin so she would not be disturbed.

We had breakfast at a stand-up bar a few blocks from the harbor — good coffee and fresh bread. Spira pointed to a toilet at the end of the room. At least I would not soil my shoes, he smiled.

After breakfast Spira took me to see a church. Along the way he pointed out some of the ruins, architecture dating back to the Romans. My sense of history was weak in this part of the world. I was surprised to learn that the Romans had ever touched this land. He went on to explain the Catholic church we were now coming to, though he was no longer a religious man himself and sensed neither was I.

"This is all," he said. I thought he was still speaking of the Roman ruins when he pushed open a door somewhere beneath a stone building. Inside it was dark except for two candles burning on a small altar. A priest in a bright green vestment was saying mass. There were no altar boys, and only three old people, two women and a man, knelt on the bare earth. There was no other sound but the priest chanting to himself.

"No young," Spira said. "No more young." We watched for a few moments, and then quietly closed the door.

At a cafe near the harbor, we drank slivovitz while I kept an eye on the ship. My wife, I hoped, was still fast asleep.

"No worry," he kept turning his head. "Hour yet," he pointed to his watch." We talked about Chicago, what the young people in America were like, literature, and art. I answered only few of his questions, laughing frequently, making extravagant gestures, which he seemed to accept and enjoy.

When the time came to leave, we shook hands, exchanged addresses, and hoped to meet someday in America or Europe. He asked me to send him some English books, and I promised him I would.

I ran, then, toward the ship, afraid any second it might move on and leave me stranded. Nothing sounded as safe as the sound of my feet hitting the stairway, rushing toward the cabin.

The tiny hallway outside our cabin was crowded with people. The door had been torn off the hinges. I found myself the center of attention — people shouting, pointing, and an officer taking my arm and leading me inside. She was sitting on the bed in her robe, sobbing hysterically and shaking her head.

She had awakened in my absence, discovered the door locked, and begun calling for me. When no one came, realizing she was not understood, she began pounding her fists on the door and screaming. An officer finally arrived, and since there was no extra key, rammed the door with his shoulder. My note had fallen somewhere under the dresser.

"Where the hell were you?"

"I told you in the note. Spira wanted us to see the city, but you were sleeping when I came in, and I thought you would rather be left alone."

"I thought you left me for good. I thought you finally decided to do it, and did it this way, locking me in a cabin and just disappearing. I thought I'd never get off this boat, never get out of this country."

"I'm sorry. Come on. Get dressed. I'll get someone to fix the door. You must be hungry. Hurry, get dressed. Look, we're moving. Let's go out on deck. Spira's probably out there watching. Split is a beautiful city, palm trees, Roman ruins. I wish you had seen it."

"When do we get to Dubrovnik?"

"Late tonight."

"Thank god we can get off this ship. It stinks. These people are like vultures."

Much later that night the ship slipped quietly into the harbor of Dubrovnik, stars showering down upon the Adriatic. Lights in the ancient fortress, flickering like candles. I stood alone on the deck earlier that evening, watching the day end, the night begin, the hood of darkness taking over the ship, the sea. As we approached Dubrovnik, the moon began its slow trek across the fortress.

At the dock an old man led us to a hotel deep within the walls of the city. We slept comfortably that night for the first time in Yugoslavia, and the next morning breakfasted on eggs and bacon, which we had not tasted since Denmark.

The day was spent discovering Dubrovnik, visiting shops where tablecloths and pillowcases were hand embroidered in the same manner as I had seen my old lady do them. And there were inlaid, hand-carved plates, utensils, and chess sets.

Dubrovnik, for me, was a poem. A poem of white stone in the afternoon sun. Old women in native costume of black skirts, embroidered vests, and white babuskas. Orange trees growing along stone streets in December. Roofs glowing in red tile along the blue sea. Everywhere you walked you felt walled-in, yet every walkway led to the sea. The sea was everywhere. The sound and sight of turquoise breakers lapping the ancient approach to the old city. Cafes with long mustachioed men playing chess, pouring rich coffee from long-handled brass pitchers set in a tray of hot sand. Peasants in the open markets selling green apples. From one courtyard to the next, walls always towering, parceling the sun and the sky. I continued to feel a freedom within walls, while my wife's shadow loomed ahead of me, searching for an opening.

I continued to find it more and more intriguing, comfortable, and wanted to settle in for a long stay. While my wife, after two days, talked of Greece and then home.

"What do you mean we can't get to Greece from here?" she exclaimed.

"There are no ships at this time of the year. Only in summer do they sail down to Piraeus from here."

"What about a train?"

"Not from here."

"Well what the hell are we going to do? You mean we have to go all the way back to Rijeka on that damn ship?"

"That's one way. Or we can take a bus part of the way, then transfer to a train bound for Belgrade. From there we can catch the Orient Express to Athens."

"Belgrade! How long will that take?"

"A couple of days. I don't know. We can take a bus to Sarajevo, then a train from there to Belgrade. But we'll have to stay overnight in Sarajevo."

"Isn't there a plane or something?"

"Probably. But it's too expensive. Don't worry. It should be very interesting. We stop in Mostar too. Mostar and Sarajevo! Who the hell would ever think we'd see such places? Nobody goes there. Turks, minarets, everything! Can you imagine being someplace like that?"

"I just want to get out of here."

"What the hell's wrong with this, tell me? What's wrong with Dubrovnik? Did anybody try to molest you? Steal from you? Do anything to you? For crissake, can't you enjoy anything?"

In less than five days we were on a bus headed for Sarajevo, only a short distance from Dubrovnik, but because of the treacherous road through the mountains, we rode for almost 10 hours. At times there was no road at all. Only paths, thousands of feet above, with no guard rails, nothing at all to protect a wheel that might slide, an old bus that might break an axle and go plummeting down with a load of people. And no one would probably even find us for days.

The bus creaked and climbed and turned for hours in a heavy rain. We stopped at least five times because of mud. But always it managed to whine its way free once again. This was Mexico all over, for me, only a thousand times worse. I was convinced we would not come out of this alive. I said nothing to my wife, tried smiling, and in the back of mind framed a small newspaper account: "Two Americans Killed in Yugoslavia."

The others on the bus, all peasants, said nothing. Every seat was filled. And there were still others sitting in the aisle. Some of the women sucked lemons to prevent motion sicknes. One old man vomited in the aisle. A child stood on the seat and peed out the window while his mother held on to him.

Some hours later we reached Mostar and stopped for lunch. My wife would not leave the bus. I went outside to get a closer view of the Mostar bridge where for me, everything was beautiful once again. The sun was out. The water flowed gently in place. And the semi-circle sweep of the bridge, completing its form in the water's reflection, was the most moving thing I had seen in all of Yugoslavia so far. A man could forget everything in Mostar. I dwelled there in peace for a long while. When I returned to the bus, someone else had taken the seat next to my wife.

I tapped the woman's shoulder and gestured that she was in my seat. I tried to explain to her that the woman at the window was my wife. But she ignored me, and no one else came to my defense. The bus started up again, and we continued on toward Sarajevo.

The mountains leveled out after Mostar. It began to rain again. It seemed, to me, that the worst of the journey was over. I stood the whole distance, bending my neck frequently to watch the hard countryside pass by. My wife, too, seemed to take an interest in the landscape for the first time. She pointed ahead to a shepherd moving his sheep down a valley. I motioned forward with my head to a peasant woman alongside the road with a tower of twigs tied to her back.

"My old lady did that when she was a girl," I explained to my wife. "She used to tell me how she would gather twigs on the mountainside for firewood, and carry a huge pile of them on her back."

"I have to go," my wife whispered to me.

"Right now?"

"Yes."

"You'll have to wait. Maybe we'll stop."

"We better."

Just before dark the bus pulled over into a grove of olive trees. Many of the people clambered off knowing somehow that this was the time and place to relieve themselves. Men and women together, stood and squatted amongst the trees. I walked with my wife, trying to find some privacy, but there seemed to be none.

"You'll just have to do what they're doing," I said.

"I'd rather do it in my pants."

"What's the difference. Look at all of them. I'll cover you as best I can."

"I don't want to look at all of them. I don't care if I ever look at any of them again. Christ, could you smell the woman sitting next to me? I'll bet she's never taken a bath in her life."

"Come on over here. Hurry, stoop down. I'll look out for you."

She squatted and hugged her knees in a way that looked like shame. I laid my hand on her head and tried to shield her from a man nearby, but another was in perfect position to watch her bare ass from the side. He smiled as she stood up and fixed herself.

Around 10 P.M. we arrived in Sarajevo. There was one taxi at the bus depot which we took to a hotel somewhere in the center of the city. I awoke early the next morning and walked for two hours through Sarajevo till my eyes suddenly began filling with tears. I kept remembering the old man.

Turks. He told me about them. And here they were. Turks all over the damn city. Feared and hated through much of thet world, yet here, Sarajevo, was a part of their heritage. They did wear fezzes still. And their pants billowed above their ankles. And some of their shoes were pointed and turned. This was a thousand and one nights. Mosques and minarets of gold and silver. A muezzin on the balcony calling to his god, calling to the streets, calling to the morning star.

The old man. I pictured him here once, long ago. Did he stand here? Know this street? Fear these Turks? What the hell was that story he once told me about his drunken friend once climbing up to the balcony and calling to Mohammed? Why the hell can't I remember all his stories?

Maybe I would leave her here as she feared I'd done in Split. She could find her way home alone. There would be money. Someone here could speak English. And I would lose myself in Sarajevo. Or go back to Mostar. Or travel to Dalmatia, find Spira, have him help me settle somewhere around there. He could help me with the visa. I could teach English, maybe, for awhile. I could write Spira from here and tell him what happened to me. I would live in Sarajevo, that's all. I would learn to speak the language. Eventually, I would make my way into Greece. Somehow.

But how the hell could I do such a thing? Could I really survive? Do I truly have the nerve? The government here would never let me stay. Not for as long as I liked. And the wife. First, her. I must get her safely back home. Then return. Perhaps from Belgrade. Fly her home from there. The Bogomils. Who were the Bogomils?

She never saw Sarajevo. And we barely spoke to each other in the short time we were there. Back from my morning's walk, we had an hour to dress, eat, and catch a taxi to the railroad station. In a first class compartment (for her sake) we kept the shades drawn and quietly rolled out of Sarajevo, comfortably, quickly to Belgrade.

Belgrade: the end. An uglines to its facade. A vague stirring to imitate the worst in western culture. I did not care to know what transpired behind the gray walls, the back streets. Nothing called me in. I stood transfixed in the center of a maze with no desire to go on. I felt her burning hate for the whole country. My telling her that Sarajevo, or Mostar, or the Dalmatian coast was Yugoslavia, would not matter. Belgrade confirmed her worst suspicions. And she wanted out.

I began to believe it myself. We were trapped. There would be no getting out of here. I moved cautiously and dazed from tourist bureau to train station looking for escape. No one spoke any English. There was only loud noise in a foreign tongue and gestures that I interpreted as delay. Markings on old schedules of trains not only seldom on time but probably non-existant.

The people seemed to know this. They waited and they waited and they waited everywhere I looked. This, to them, was hope.

The train station. I should not have taken her there that day. I was tired, and growing frightened, of walking streets, visiting offices, meeting only deadends. I asked her to come with me, to talk to one of the clerks at the station while I talked to another.

The place had become crowded with people overnight. There were no trains, none the day before. Yet the people kept coming, all of them headed somewhere, all of them moving almost instinctively into the station, waiting for trains. The station began to overflow with men, women and children. They filled the benches, the floors, and then the sidewalks outside.

We began stepping over them, stepping, at times, on hands and feet. People punched us in the leg as we waded through this wretched sea of humanity toward the clerk's window. And when we got there, it was closed.

The people, dressed mostly in black, stretched out on the floors and tried to sleep. They were huddled along the platforms and even along the tracks. Policemen and soldiers moved among them, tapping them with clubs, making them sit up, stand up, stay awake. Women breast-fed their babies. Men drank from large bottles.

Then the sound of a whistle.

People crawling to their feet. The mass of them pushing toward the tracks. My wife and I engulfed, separated by their maddening crush to get closer to the train. Arms and fists swinging. My raincoat ripped from my back. My jacket pulled off of me . . . money, passport . . . gone. A loudness of language erupting in screams.

The light of the engine, the steam, the iron ugliness of it all approaching in slow movement. People scrambling from the track. Screams. Somebody possibly hit, or surely trampled upon.

There was no chance of our boarding that train. There were only two passenger cars. People hanging from the window, the steps, the engine itself as it began to back out. People hurling bottles and stones at the engineers. Fifty empty cars would not have been enough to take all of the people left waiting.

"Even the Turk won't get out," she said on our way back to the hotel.

"What Turk?"

"The Turk in the hotel. The Turk who began crying when he talked to me. Someone will kill him, he said."

"What the hell are you talking about?"

"The Turk drives a Mercedes, and it has broken down three times since he entered this country from Italy. He should have gone another way. He knows that now. There is no short cut through this country. Each time the car breaks down it take the Turk a week to find a mechanic. Now there are no more mechanics. There are no mechanics for Turks in Belgrade. So they will kill him. They will take his Mercedes, and they will kill the Turk."

"Fuck the Turk. I'll get you out of here."

"Fuck the Turk. Cut off his head. Axe him in half. Fuck the Turk!" And she began to laugh.

"You're beginning to sound just like me."

A block from our hotel, just ahead of us on the street, a crowd had gathered. "It's the Turk," I kidded her. "They just killed him."

A man had cornered a boy in a doorway, and people watched on as he held the boy by the wrists and beat him on the head with his fist. He was bleeding from the eyes and nose when I saw the man grab two fingers of the boy's hand and bend them back. They snapped like dry twigs and hung there by the skin.

A soldier beside me answered my wife's scream, my own fearful questioning of the faces around me . . . "What did he do? What's wrong?"

"Thief," the soldier smiled. "Father teach."

I remember both holding and hitting my own wife. Knocking her down to the pavement to control the hysteria. As if attacking her somehow freed me and the boy. I remember struggling with the soldier. My wife curled at my feet, screaming. I remember running. Leaving her bleed on the streets of Belgrade, leaving her to the embassy, to her mother to make arrangements for her safe return. I remember running off, quite madly, to find the tombs of the Bogomils.

Spira? Where are they, Spira? Where are those fucking childish stones of running deer and birds? Who were the Bogomils, Spira? Help me. Who were they? This is my father's contry. I have to know what it means to me. Tell me, Spira. Teach me Dragats' epitaph . . .

> Here lies Dragats
> When I wished to be,
> I ceased to be.

Fuck the Turk!

I boarded a bus that took me to Skopje where someone saw me wandering the streets, put me in a jail or hospital . . . unclaimed. And finally shipped me back to America all wrapped up and smelling of death.

Hassock, that's me.
"What is your real name?"
Hassock.
"Who is the President of the United States?"
Wenceslaus.
"What do you do?"
Nothing.
"They say you're an artist. A teacher? A writer?"
To do something with love.
"Did you love your wife? Did you try to kill her?"
I did?
"She put you here for help. You are separated from her."
I'm separate.
"Don't you like the looks of yourself in the mirror?"
I don't see myself.
"You just got a shave and a haircut. You look respectable again."
Look at me.
"What's your name?"

Fuck you.

"You're being childish. How old are you?"

My pubic hair is growing gray. There is no resurrection. Et cum spiritu tuo.

"Your mother is dead, you know. She died in a place like this some weeks ago."

It's all dying.

"And your father is not well. His heart will not hold out. He had an accident. A fall from a ladder."

My father is a muzzin in a minaret in Mostar. Alliteration. He carries blocks of ice to the balcony and drops them. My father, the iceman.

"Do you remember your mother and father? Nurse . . ."

This place smells like her, where we took her. We left her in a room and we sat outside and then they told us to come in and the room was big like this with tile brick walls and cold filled with beds with white metal bars, full of crazy people dressed in white, the nurse was black and white, white doctor, white pills. And the lady in the chair who pissed and pissed and pissed. That young girl who called me a prick, hey you prick. And that one at the end of the room who growled. The fat woman all uncovered with her cunt shaved and bristly, and the hair under her nose and around her ass and she moved the whole bed fighting the straps and growling and growling. It smelled the same, I remember.

"I understand you and your father put her in a state hospital for help . . ."

They took her out of the trial room finally because she couldn't answer any questions like who is the President of the United States? She was on trial, and when she couldn't answer the questions, they undressed her and put her in white and gave us a paper bag with her old clothes in it and the old man took them home and burned them in the alley that night.

"It won't be long and you'll be out of here. You should begin thinking about that. Maybe a little manual labor at first. The outdoors. Put the mind at rest for awhile. Get the soul in order, as they say. Then maybe try a little teaching again. You're not a bad off as you think you are. Your father could use your help. Listen to me, goddamn it! I'm going to kick your ass out of here, do you understand? I'm throwing you back out in the cold fucking world! You're a phony madman. I know the act. The state can't afford such theater. You're not dangerous at all. Angry, maybe. You couldn't hurt a goddam thing, including yourself. You don't even have the guts to *think* about killing yourself. Whatever the hell you are, you still have time to find out."

Part III

No was the night. Yes is this present sun.
It can never be satisifed, the mind, never.
—Wallace Stevens

Hexagram 41

Sun Loss, Reduction

This hexagram symbolizes a
marshy lake at the foot of a mountain. The Superior Man keeps his
anger under control and is moderate in his desires.

Part III

Part III . . .

"Hello, Blazen?"

"Hassock, here."

"Blazen, it's me, Reckelson, remember? Campbell City High? I heard you got back sometime ago and were looking for a teaching job."

"Well, Reckelson, you sonofabitch. You sound as sinister as ever."

"Cut the sinister shit, buddy. I'm here to lend you a hand. Schauk called me. Some doctor or somebody called him, some guy you were working with, and wondered if you might be able to get back into Campbell High. It's no soap there. Nowhere to go. I left a year ago myself. Schauk's still there. Same as ever. The entertainer, you know. I tried to spring him, but no luck. He'll die there. I'm trying to get the best teachers I can lay my hands on for the system I'm in now. It may be too late for Schauk, but not you. You're young yet. Flexible. And if you really want to teach, I can help you out. I'm co-chairman of the English department here at North Highland High."

"Where the hell's that?"

"New suburban area on the westside of Chicago. Not too far from you. In fact, you probably passed the area on your way to Campbell every morning. It'll be a lot closer for you."

"You mean where they were digging along the expressway, near the cloverleaf?"

"Yeah, That's it. We're right by the cloverleaf in fact. I can see it from my office window, just right of the flagpole."

"Nice location."

"You're damn right. And good people. You know what I mean? Not like the Campbell City riff-raff. Upper-middle class here. And upper. Most of the parents are college graduates. The fathers, corporate executives, scientists, big-time sales representatives. They back the school system a hundred precent. A fringe of working class people too, but for the most part, intelligent, hard working Americans who want the best for their children."

"I've heard that before. Listen, Reckelson, it's nice you called and everything, especially since we were never real good friends, but you don't want me. I'm separated or divorced or something. I just got out of the funny farm. I'm living with my sick and dying old man on Social Security, pension, stuff like that. I can barely maneuver around here, let alone try to make my way around a clasroom again. I don't remember a goddam thing about education, or even why we do it in 'school systems.' I'd be nothing but trouble. I don't even think I'm certified anymore. Certified crazy, maybe. But not a certified teacher."

"Listen. I trust you. We'll take care of that."

"I could be dangerous . . . who knows? You're right, I do need a job. But what the fuck would that community want with me? If I was 'lower class' at Campbell, what the hell will they think of me in Highland?"

"Don't worry. We need fresh ideas, youth, a good teacher. Someone who has the potential of becoming a good teacher. I want to cultivate that kind of person; that's why I do all the recruiting for the English department here. Your file speaks for itself, Blazen."

"Hassock."

"Why, Hassock?"

"Because I feel comfortable with it."

"Your files are in good shape. I mean, as far as college is concerned, and your recommendations. Somebody even said that you would one day be a master teacher."

"Who?"

"I'm not supposed to reveal that. Confidential information."

"Who the fuck was it, Reckelson?"

"A Professor Addur."

"How the hell did he get into my files? God bless you, Addur."

"The Campbell City recommendations — not so hot. I'll have to bury most of those. Don't worry. It will all be in order here when I talk to Walt Scutters, the principal."

"What the hell time is it, Reckelson? Where are we? What month? I've been pushing concrete for the last few months or so and today I dumped a full wheelbarrow on top of one of the bricklayers. Is this September or what?"

"The first of November. Now here's the deal. Since I'm associate chairman, I have only one class a day. Sounds like a piece of cake, but I don't even have time to do one class justice with all the organizing going on here. So I told Meeks, the chairman, my co-chairman, that I need more time to get this department in gear. So we talked with the principal, Scutters, about hiring a permanent substitute to take over this one class a day. Now, they've got a woman in mind who hasn't taught in 15 years. One of those deals where all the kids are gone and the husband works all day and the woman is bored with nothing to do. Well, I kind of put the lid on her because of physical disability, she limps. So you're it, you see? I've already sold you to Meeks. And Scutters I'll show Addur's recommendation. So you should be all set. How would you like to be back in the classroom on next Monday?"

"What about all that time lost in between teaching? How do I explain that?"

"You were traveling. And you're an artist, a young writer or something, aren't you? That's the tickey, isn't it?"

"Tell me, Reckelson, how come you weren't my friend before?"

"That's what I like about you, Blazen, a sense of humor."

"Hassock."

"All right, Hassock. You always did have a sense of humor. Your kids told me. So did Schauk. It'll be great to have you on our staff. And Highlands will be good to you, believe me."

"Just leave me alone, Reckelson. That's all I ask. Only one class, huh?"

"For a start. A chance to get back in shape. I'll get you good money, don't worry. Do a good job, Hassock, and next September you'll have a full-time schedule: four classes and a study hall. Four good classes. No dunderheads. No discipline problems."

"What am I teaching?"

"A great class! Mine. A special deal — since I'm co-chairman. It's a snap, Hassock. Only nine kids in American literature. Nine damn good kids, college-bound. I've got them all broken in for you. They're readers. They come from good homes. They still need some drill work in grammar, but you can handle it, I know. All 'A' and 'B' students and maybe one or two 'C's. They'll do anything you ask. And do it well. Plenty of room for discussion time, if you want. They like to talk along those lines. Five girls and four boys. All-American."

"You mean no blacks."

"Yeah, that's right, Hassock! We've got a few, but they're in special classes."

"What's the text?"

"We have our own grammar book, a handbook which I put together. I'm into restrictive clauses now. You can begin with non-restrictive on Monday, or begin with literature, if you like."

"What's the text?"

"*Adventures in American Literature.* Know it? You must."

"Yeah, I believe I do."

"I usually begin with 'The Growth of American Literature' . . . the Colonial period. But feel free to start with the modern, if you like, and work backwards. See you on Monday then. The class starts at 10:10, my room #127. It's at the end of the first ray. Come early so you can meet Walt Scutters and Ken Meeks and the rest of the gang. Department meeting on Wednesday, 3:15. You'll have to stick around or come back for that. I'll introduce you to everybody then, Blazen."

"Just call me Hassock."

And so . . . Here comes, there goes Hassock. Leaving home, the old neighborhood now, the front basement of the old man's bungalow. The old man himself slightly asleep upstairs, slightly out of it.

Go to sleep, old man. Rest. I've dialed "the Bohemian Hour" on the radio. Listen. Lots of polkas. Dance, old man, dance. Polka in your head all the way to the grave.

Here goes Hassock, me, looking at himself. Riding the west-bound blue bus that will take him to North Highland each morning. Look at Hassock by the window wearing a flannel shirt, striped tie, perma-press Levis, gum-soled workshoes, and a black lunchbox in his lap. He studies, in earnest, a dirty book (he has not had much lately), *The Green-Eyed Nympho:*

> Both were now worked up to a fever pitch and neither wanted further delay. Armond broke their embrace and Nancy sank to the couch. She quickly swung her legs up on it and then lay back and separated them. She raised her knees in the age-old invitation and held out her arms to him . . .

Hassock nurtures a hardon for those age-old invitations. The bus stops on a hill near the cloverleaf, and it's off to work and down the hill with Hassock, swinging his lunchbox — holding a Thermos of coffee, a sweetroll, a pencil, and *The Green-Eyed Nympho* — off to school.

9 a.m. of a November morning. The kids already inside, the sun shining, the eyes blinded, the school, North Highland High, a veritable glasshouse/greenhouse wheel with spokes of classrooms radiating into the streets, the houses of suburbia. In the center, soaring straight-white, onwards and upwards, a flagpole. Old Glory waving to beat hell. Hello, America, here comes Hassock, your native son.

There he goes into the central glass cylinder, getting lost in concentric circles of offices, glass classrooms. See him ask his way to the teacher's cafeteria? See him sway down Ray #1, open a wooden door: TEACHERS LOUNGE: ENGLISH DEPARTMENT ONLY. Hear him holler:

"Reckelson, where the fuck are you?"

114

"Hassock! Good to see you, old man. Where's your suit coat? Come on, have some coffee. Most of the English people have classes this hour, but there are a few people here you should meet. Carol Skyes, I want you to meet a good friend of mine, ah, Hassock."

"Hassock? That's a peculiar name."

"Where did you get such green eyes?"

"And, Hassock, this is Mike Clay over here, Cynthia Ellsworth, and that's about it for now."

"Cheers."

"Hassock, maybe you and I ought to have a few private words first, and then we'll join the gang. Excuse us, please. No, sit over there in the corner. You mean they still make those lunch buckets? I haven't seen one in years."

"That's because you haven't been pushing concrete."

"Well, what do you think of the place so far? A beautiful plant, isn't it? A sign of things to come education-wise. A feeling of the outside, with all this glass, don't you think?"

"Tell me more about Carol and Cynthia."

"Ah, Hassock, you're a riot. No time for games now. Listen, everything's set. Meeks gave you the OK and said he'll try to see you sometime this week. As far as Scutters is concerned, he's a hard man to find. Busier than hell, which I'm sure you can appreciate. But he did see your records, probably made a few phone calls, and gave me the OK on you this morning. I'm sure you'll meet him, and like him, before long.

He's a straight shooter."

"Fuck him. I have no use for administrators. I've learned that."

"Be careful of the language, buddy. Even though this is 'department only' territory, you never know. Where the hell's your suit coat? Don't you have a sport jacket or something?"

"No."

"Well I'll loan you some bucks. See if you can pick up something this afternoon."

"I like what I've got on. I'm comfortable. I bought a dozen of these shirts while making my career in concrete. There's even a little opening here for my pencil, see? I'll bet you don't have one on your shirt pocket."

"I don't know how this is going to go over. Just keep a low profile."

"I intend to. There's an outside door to every classroom, isn't there?"

"Yes. A safety measure."

"Just be sure mine's open every morning about 10, and I'll enter and exit that way. Don't want to cause you or anyone any embarrassment."

115

"You know I don't mean it that way, buddy. Dress anyway you like; it's a free country. Within reason, of course . . ."

"Ah, reason. There's the rub."

"The kids make their own dress code here. Levis are iffy. Skirts, even with the knees. As long as you wear a tie, it should be okay."

"You're a nice guy, Reckelson. How come you weren't my friend at Campbell City?"

"Forget that place. Here's your gradebook, seating chart, class list, lesson plan book, spelling list of The 100 Most Misspelled Words — quiz them every Friday on these — *Grammatical Constructions for Life,* which I put together myself, and *Adventures In American Literature.* And here's a key to room #127, and another key for the file cabinet. Always keep your file cabinet locked, don't forget. The room, which I sort of use as an office until my new one is ready in the main circle, is yours almost any time. You can have the bottom drawer of the desk. Feel free to have the kids in for consultation before school, after school, after class, anytime. Okay?"

"Carol's staring at me."

"She's a good kid. Masters from Northwestern in reading skills. Likes her gin and tonic every Friday after school. You'll like her."

"Will she go to bed with me?"

"Hassock, you're some character. Were you like this at Campbell? I don't remember. We never had the chance to talk much. Come on, we've got a few minutes left. Let's go join the gang."

"Well, Mr. Hassock, are you all set to take command?"

"Hassock, green-eyes. Just Hassock."

"Where did you get that funny looking outfit, and the flannel shirt, Mr. Hassock?" asks Mr. Clay.

"Where'd you get that white shirt with the yellow collar?"

"You're all right, Hassock," laughs Clay. "I'm gonna get me one of those shirts myself."

"What were you involved in prior to coming to Highland?" questions syllably perfect Miss Ellsworth, teacher of speech.

"Women. Once there was a wife . . . Always women. I carried mail to them every day for a few weeks, right after I graduated from the State Institution. I brought them messages of love and death, mostly death. Then my legs gave out. Then I pushed concrete till my arms fell off. I lost my wheelbarrow one sunny morning, buried a bricklayer from the old country, Anton, in concrete. Couldn't understand the sonofabitch anyway. Before that I was a traveling man, my own circus. Those who can, do. Before that I tried teaching I think."

116

"Yes," says Reckelson, clearing his throat. "He's quite a world traveler and has done some writing, a book in progress, I hear."

"Oh, that explains it. An author. The costume, I mean," chortles Miss Ellsworth.

"Miss Ellsworth, do you read lips? Read mine . . ."

"Ah, there goes the bell," Reckelson jumps to his feet. "We better be going, Hassock. I'll introduce you to the class, and then they're all yours. We'll see the rest of you people later."

"So long, Hassock," Clay thrusts a meaty hand. "You're going to be just fine."

"Bye, Hassock. Good luck. I'll see you around," bids Carol Skyes.

"Auuug," moans Hassock. "Miss Ellsworth didn't even say goodbye."

Room #127 . . . the end of the first glass ray and just across the hall from the department lounge. The Bell has Rung. The Bell has Rung. The Bell has Rung indeed. The bell tolls for thee, Hassock.

Everyone in his and her seat. Hassock, his back to the class, his hands in his back pockets, his black lunchbox hanging from the thumb of his right hand . . . Hassock studying diagrams of non-restrictive clauses on the greenboard. (What *are* these fuckers?) Reckelson standing by the lectern, enthused. No more teaching; goodbye class. Off to the inner circles of administration. Today, co-chairman; tomorrow, principal? superintendent?

"The bell has rung, class. As you all know, today is my last day with you, much to my regret." (Moans . . . truly genuine sighs of regret. Hassock is moved.) "Yes, I know. Believe me, I'll miss you people too. I've really enjoyed this class even though we've been together such a short time. But I'm sure you will also get on well with your new teacher, a fine man, and an old colleague of mine. He has taught for a number of years, travelled in many parts of the world, and returned sometime ago from the Middle East, or Eastern Europe, I believe. He has a keen interest in literature and writing, and I know you're going to learn much from him. Well, I better stop talking and get moving and give you people the time to get better acquainted. You had a final assignment today on non-restrictive clauses. Please hand those in at the end of the hour. We'll give your new teacher some homework tonight. (Laughter . . . kids joining in.) And I've put more examples of non-restrictive clauses on the board to study and discuss today. Okay, Mr. Hassock, they're all yours."

Hassock turns, smiles, drops his lunchbox on the desk, shakes hands with Reckelson as the kids applaud, and shout goodbye. Followed by silence as Hassock closes the door behind Reckelson. Nine faces, alphabetically up and down the two center rows. He looks at their faces; they study his. He pulls the chair from the desk and sits down. The big red hand on the clock moves slowly with an electric hum and a bounce . . . 3 . . . 4 . . . 5 . . .6 . . .

"Sir, what did Mr. Reckelson say your name was?"

"Hassock. Just Hassock."

"Would you put it on the board?"

"No."

More silence. A hand.

"Mr. Hassock, could you please explain the diagrams on the board?"

"Hassock. Just Hassock. What's your name?"

"Jack Smith."

"And yours?" Hassock pointing at random, his feet now upon the desk.

"Kirstin Wilkinson," "Gloria Bywater," "Nick Tarble," "Diane Gurbal," "Karl Hinds," "Emma Ashbridge," "Marvin Berger," "Joy Ginn."

"Thank you. Nice names . . . especially 'Joy Ginn.' Nice sound to it. I think names are important, don't you?" (Silence.) You don't, huh? Well, anyway, I sort of like my name, Hassock. Jack, tell me about yourself."

"I'm a junior. A straight A student. I plan to major in chemistry and physics in college."

"Tell me, Jack, is there a Jill? I mean, what do you do for fun?"

"Well, I'm usually kind of busy for any social life. I'm in the young people's church group. And I play in the orchestra. I like to read."

"How about you, Joy?"

"I'm a cheerleader, and ah . . ."

"Mostly boom-a-lay-boom-a-lay, boom-a-lay boom, huh?" (laughter.) "Sort of . . ."

"Mr. Hassock?"

"Hassock, Jack. Just Hassock."

"I don't feel comfortable calling you Hassock."

"Well I won't answer to anything else."

"Hassock, what about the diagrams, the non-restrictive clauses? Would you explain those please?"

"I wish I could, but I don't really understand them myself. Grammar has always been a bit of a mystery to me."

Laughter. A guffaw from a dark, round, happy-faced kid named Nick Tarble.

"What's so funny, Nick?"

"You. You don't understand this stuff and you expect us to and you're

118

supposed to be an English teacher."

"Don't believe everything English teachers tell you. Don't believe in English teachers, in fact. Nobody knows everything about English, believe me. *That* you can believe. Take the answer book away from an English teacher, and there you will find innocence. Now Reckelson here, your old English teacher, you all remember him, don't you? Well Reckelson left me a copy of *Grammatical Constructions for Life,* but he's got all the answers. He took them with him, you see. Why, hell, he wrote the book! But we don't need his answers. We're talking, ain't we? We're *communicating.* You understand me, and I understand you. Why take the whole damn language apart to see how it works? When something doesn't work, when it breaks down, then you take it apart and attempt to repair it. Well, everything seems in good working order here, as far as I can tell. And there *are* more important things to be concerned in living, literally or otherwise."

"But Mr. Hassock?"

"Hassock, Gloria."

"Hassock, what about composition? The college board exams. We have to know how to write well, and proper usage is a big part of it. My mother was a teacher, and she keeps telling me this all the time."

"Yes. True. More or less. Believe what you want to believe for the time being. I don't want to get into all of this right now. I'll buy some notebooks for you tomorrow. The notebooks are on me. And you start writing in them. Write about everything and mostly yourself. Tell me stories, write me letters, poems, anything. Even draw some pictures if you like. Tell me the true things about yourselves. Try not to show any of this to your parents. This is your own. It's private. It's between you and me and nobody else. And write in a way that seems most natural to you. And don't worry about spelling, or punctuation, or grammar. That can come later. For now just enjoy what you write. Whatever we are doing, whatever you are doing, thinking, feeling, observing, write about it. Anything I should say or do or suggest, you try your own hand at it. I'll collect all the notebooks every so often; I'll read everything you've written. We'll take it from there. And for the time being, we'll skip this formal grammar business."

"But won't we be behind?" chirps Emma Asbridge . . . brain, brain, brain, written all over her smart-alecky face.

"Behind what?"

"Behind the other classes. We surely can't skip the entire grammar unit and expect to keep up with the other classes, let alone take the final, departmental exam."

"Did somebody get ahead of us? I didn't realize that. Is there a race toward that big non-restrictive clause in the sky? You're only juniors. Don't worry about any exam. I'll give you the answers, if you like. College will always be there. It's no big deal anyway. Colleges don't matter. High schools don't matter. English and grammar doesn't even matter. Teachers matter. They're all that counts. If you have one great teacher in your lifetime, it could make all the difference."

"What about homework papers?" asks Jack.

"What about them?"

"Aren't you supposed to grade them? Mr. Reckelson always collected them at the end of the hour and returned them the next day with our grades."

"Okay, okay. Let's get this straight. Mr. Reckelson is dead. We buried him in the main circle. And he will not be resurrected. My name is Hassock, and I'm your teacher to the end. What Reckelson did was Reckelson's way. And that's over. What's important now is Hassock's way. Throw those homework papers in the wastebasket."

"What's for tomorrow?"

"You are ... ah ... Marvin, Marvin Berger. Nothing. I have no plans for tomorrow just as I had no plans for today. Just be here. I did say I would have some notebooks for you. We'll just have to see, and take it from there."

"Hassock?"

"Yes, Emma."

"You're going to be in trouble. Everyone is supposed to have at least a half-hour of homework a night for each class."

"I won't assign homework. You decide that for yourself. You study because you want to study, because you're interested in what we say or do in class. That's the only kind of homework that matters. I say go read some John Steinbeck, and you go ahead and read three novels of Steinbeck because you discovered you liked what he had to say, and how he said it. Please erase the board, will you Emma? That you. Yes? Your name?"

"Karl Hinds. Ah, this is Monday morning, Hassock. And the first five minutes are supposed to be sort of a homeroom where you read the weekly bulletin and everything. And we're supposed to say the Pledge of Allegiance, and we haven't said it yet."

"You mean they do that in high school now? Well, go ahead. Do it."

"You're supposed to lead us."

"Truthfully, I don't quite remember it all because they changed it or something, didn't they? Didn't they stick God in somewhere? Where's the flag?"

"Right above your head."

"Right, Jack. Lead on, will you?"

"Everybody stand and face the flag, please. I pledge allegiance . . ."

And there goes Hassock, walking around the room, mumbling to himself. His hand half-heartedly rubbing his chest, his eyes searching out the two girls he hasn't heard from yet: Diane Gurbal and Kirstin Wilkinson. Beautiful girl, Kirstin, Ugh, Gurbal. Fat. Acne. Thick nyloned legs stuffed in a pair of white tennis shoes. Nylons wrinkled around the ankles . . . "with liberty and justice for all. Sit down. Sit down. I don't see any bulletin around here, so I guess there's no news today. Any questions? Okay, class dismissed."

"We have to wait for the bell," says Jack.

"Oh. Okay. Well, wait for it. But I'm gonna cut. I'll see you guys tomorrow."

Here goes Hassock out his getaway door, lunchbox swinging. 11 o'clock in the morning, free! "I think I'm learning," he says to himself.

Busing it back to the neighborhood. An afternoon of bed, doing nothing, forgetting everything, waiting for mail, keeping a watch on the old man upstairs. Sleeping, drinking, eating, reading, writing, loving — if possible. Hassock in the basement on a bed piled high with books, newspapers, magazines, ash trays, beer cans, coffee cups, and his lunchbox beside him: *The Green-Eyed Nympho* —

> Craning her neck, she peered through the semi-darkness to
> see what the other couples were doing. Ruth, it seemed,
> had become highly aroused by the film, and at the moment
> was grasping her partner intimately in one hand, while he
> was busily engaged in unbuttoning her dress . . .

"Ohhhhhhhhh," agony from the upstairs. The old man in bed, body all achin' and racked with pain. Hassock grabbing a broom and signaling with the handle against the ceiling — boom, boom, boom — that he was there/here, just below, on duty. Day watch. Night watch. Death watch. Boom, boom, boom. I'll be right up.

Up the backstairs he goes. Into the icebox for two beers. Into the linen closet, tearing off another piece of the old lady's hand-embroidered sheet, making a diaper for dad, should he need it.

Into the bedroom. "Ohhhhhhhhh." Yeah, yeah, yeah. Hassock himself still filled with love and hate for the sad figure of a man lying there. See what you get for fucking around with ladders at your age, old man? Ask the Sacred Heart on the wall to help you. Fix the house, fix the gutters, fix the windows. The house fixed you. Tell it to the guy on the crucifix over your head. Or the one with his heart out on the wall and no holy water in the well. Here's some holy water for us, old man. From Chief Sacred Heart: I bless you in the name of my mother, of me, of all the mystery. Drink up, old man. Who's going to go up and paint the gutters after you're gone? Not Crazy Son, that's for sure. If stroke does me in, let it be the sun. Not this. Do you need a change? Can I help you to the bathroom?

What? What are you saying? The radio? Oh, I forgot to put the Bohemian Hour on this morning. I see. I'm sorry. I'm working now, regular. New start. Teaching again. A brand new life. I'll move that heavy bastard of a console TV in here for you this afternoon. You can watch that when I'm gone. I'm gonna take good care of you. I'm gonna make liver dumpling soup for supper just like the old lady used to make. Here, take another swig. Shot? You want a shot? Wait, I'll see what's left. Here, I'll split it with you. That's all. I'll put that on my shopping list. Feeling good? What the hell. What else can happen, huh? We got the bull by the horns.

Yeah, I started teaching again. Today. Just one class. A good bunch of kids. I'm going to give it one more try. There's a lot to learn about kids. You never knew much about this. Teaching is a very dangerous thing. So is fathering, I'm sure. I don't want to make too many mistakes. Well, I'm going back down to read. Holler if you need anything. I'll be up later with something to eat. Here's the radio.

Hassock jumping down the backstairs, two-at-a-time, two-at-a-time, through the rear of the basement, tools, saws, rakes, shovels, ladders, cans of paint, washing machine, old shoes and clothes, wooden wagon, cement wash tubs and a pile of dirty laundry on the floor, ice box, ice tongs, a row of plants (Mother-in-law Tongue) . . . got to water those bastards some day . . . Tide, Rinso, workbench, hot water heater, furnace, little sewer hole in the floor . . . door . . . Hassock's home!

Creaky bedsprings. Slug of beer. *The Green-Eyed Nympho.* Hassock has lost his place. Opening it, anywhere . . .

> Her own date for the evening was obviously caught up in the animal passion that prevailed in the room, and his hands were now roaming over her body with increasing abandon. She was just about to protest his advances, when suddenly the room was plunged into total darkness . . .

Hassock dropping off to sleep.

"We missed you at the department meeting the other afternoon, Hassock."

"How come you're so fucking subtle, Reckelson? How come you corner me in the lounge every morning?"

"Shhh. Watch the language. There are women present."

"One woman and one bitch."

"If you stayed around here a little longer in the afternoon, I could introduce you to some of the others. In fact, you could have met them all at the meeting last Wednesday. I introduced you, thinking you were there, the department's so large, and it was very embarrassing for me when you didn't stand up. I felt very foolish."

"That's part of the profession. The question is, were they laughing at you or me? Anyway, department meetings just confuse me. Let's go sit over there with those folks."

"One minute. I've got a few more things to clear up with you. I brought one of these brown folders for you with your name on it. The staff finds it handy. Keep your gradebook in it, your manila folders, papers to grade, just about everything. Like a briefcase. It has a nice elastic band around it to keep everything tight. I requisitioned 3 red felt tip pens for you, they're in there. And, let's see: paper clips, 1 box; rubber bands, 2 dozen; Scotch tape, 1 reel; 3x5 notecards, 1 package; 3 pencils, #2 soft; and a small bottle of Elmer's Glue. If you need anything else, let me know. I'll leave some order forms for you in the bottom desk drawer."

"Who do I write a thank you note to for all this?"

"The Board. The taxpayers. The department. No digging into your own pocket for supplies here. And there's no need to go without anything. Just fill out the order for materials, and you shall receive. Now, one other thing. Two memos came down to me today. One from Meeks, the other from Scutters. They both concern a rumor about you. A parent is concerned because you haven't been assigning any homework. This is an exceptional high school, Hassock. We have a high number of National Merit students. The parents expect their kids to go on to the Big 10 colleges and even the Ivy League. They want these kids to be ready. They expect the teachers to work the kids hard, and what's more, the kids themselves expect to be worked hard! It's not Campbell City, Hassock. I told you that. Get your ass in gear. I talked to one of your kids, and he told me you weren't doing much in class, just a lot of talking. A lot of ideas. Now some of that's all right. But it's basics, Hassock. Basics! Remember, I got you in here as a favor. It's my ass as well as yours. I know you've got responsibilities at home and everything, your father isn't very well, but you have work to do here. Don't forget that. Meeks wants to visit your class sometime soon."

"What's he like?"

"A nice guy. You'll like him. He likes sincerity in people. I'm sure he's going to like you."

"I don't want the sonofabitch near my class. I can't concentrate with those characters in my classroom. You know what happened to me at Campbell? Just keep him the hell away from me when I'm trying to teach. Let me run the show, will you? There's a lot I want to try and do. Those guys spook me."

"What can I do? He's the chairman of the department? He goes where he wants to go."

"Well I'll lock the bastard out. If he wants to talk, I'll talk to him in here, or in his office, or over a beer somewhere. I'm here to teach, not to be observed. Let the kids judge at the end of the year. If they say Hassock is a half-ass teacher, Hassock will leave. I've got no time for administrative assholes, whatever their titles. I'm just starting to bring the class around. Trust me, Reckelson. There will be a lot of good surprises."

"What the hell do you want me to do? What if I sit-in for him and turn in an evaluation? You've got to be evaluated. Would that work?"

"You just turn in the evaluation and pretend you observed. Or let me turn it in. It's my class. My business. My ass."

"Your ass? What about mine? No, Hassock, there's where you're wrong. You better learn this now. The school belongs to the community. Don't ever forget that. We represent them. We *work* for them! And we play by their rules. And their rules state that to maintain efficiency, optimum performance in the classroom, teachers must be evaluated. Tenure after two years probation. They want no dead wood around here."

"I guess it depends on how you define dead wood. I'd say they're guaranteeing more of the same."

"Listen. It's going to be all right. It's only your first week. Give the system a chance. How about lunch tomorrow with me and Meeks?"

"Can't. I've got a father to look after. I can get a neighbor to look in once in a while, but that costs. And I have to set it up a few days in advance."

"Well, another time. Oh, one more thing. I forgot to mention that in the main office, in the first circle, you know? There's a section there for teachers' boxes. You should check that every day, first thing in the morning for weekly bulletins, notes, announcements, memos, mail and other things. I had your name put on one of the boxes in the last row. You're out of alphabetical order for the time being. You're at the end, after the 'Z's'. After the cafeteria and custodial personnel. So keep an eye on the box, will you?"

"What?"

"Box."

"I've got my eye on it right now. Hey, Green-eyes! Care to share a cookie from my lunchbox?"

"Hassock, you horny bastard. Now don't forget."

"Okay. I'll see you. Hey, Green-eyes, I'm coming with your cookie."

"Hi, Hassock. Sit down, you dirty old man. Cookies . . ."

"Well, it works with dirty old men and little girls, I've been told."

"Hassock . . ."

"Hey, hello, Clay. I've just been trying to lay a, no!, lure a lady here with some cookies."

"You're disgusting," says Miss Ellsworth. "Grow up."

"You know, she's right. I feel like a kid back in high school again. It must be the administrative atmosphere. By the way, Miss Ellsworth, can you help me? I have a speech problem. It seems every other word I pronounce seems to come out sounding like 'fuck'. Wait, wait! Don't go, Elsie."

"Hassock, you crazy sonofabitch," says Clay, removing his glasses, rubbing his eyes.

"That's all right, Green-eyes. You can laugh too. No harm. Here, I brought a cookie for each of us. Let's raise our cups to Elsie. Tell me something, teachers, what's this guy Meeks like? He's planning to do an evaluation job on me."

"Well," says Carol Skyes, "He's a fairy nice man, if you know what I mean."

"He takes thancing lessons," says Clay.

"Oh, no, no. How come? Home come these guys are always in English? Are male English teachers all latent homosexuals, huh, Clay? How come there's seldom anyone with balls teaching English? There goes the bell."

"Balls," says Clay.

"Ditto," says Green-eyes.

"When shall we three meet again?" says Hassock.

"How about two," says Green-eyes. "Just me and you. Clay's married and a moral man. And on the wagon. Oh, I'm sorry. Clay. I pray for your fall once again."

"That's okay. That's okay. I'm just trying to lead a normal, decent life again."

"After school, Friday?" says Hassock.

"I'll sleep on it," smiles Green-eyes. "I'll leave a note in your box."

"Wish I had said that, Clay."

Friday. The class is over. Hassock assigns: The burial of *Grammatical Constructions for Life,* 10 copies, neatly stacked, in the waste basket. Hassock next awaits the afternoon. The sound of the bell, wrapping everyone in classrooms once again. Then, Hassock on the move, side-stepping and dodging it down the glass ray, lunchbox swinging, making himself fearfully acquainted with the High School Plant. Moving in on that main circle then suddenly rocketing down another ray at the sight of anyone looking administrative. He knows their walk, their dress, their gaze. Box, box, box, echoes Hassock. Got to find the box, the meaning inside, Green-eyes. Silence. Hassock toe-tipping into the first circle. He spies Reckelson's face smeared on a pane of glass, turns suddenly one way then another. Into another ring of offices, secretaries electrically pecking away in their white-on-white Lady Manhattan shirts. Bong! TILT. A mean man with yellow teeth coming on strong with a stack of manila folders. Hassock slides right? left? up? No, down. A door dealing in DOWN. So down the spiral staircase Hassock descends, down, down, down in the dark, the tips of his shoelaces tinkling the metal stairs. Light? A little light? Cylinders and pipes, the feeling of pressure, of steam . . . inferno? Boiler room! A tiny red light bulb and the hulk of a man eating at a table. The man shines a flashlight at the dark stairs.

"Who dat?"

"Me, Hassock?"

"Ha Cock?"

"Yeah, The new man. Teacher."

"How come you no look like teacher? You look like new man suppose to come today take care boiler room. Me go vacation sometime. No work forever. Break in new man today, part-time. Ha Cock?"

"Hassock."

"Slovak?"

"Sort of."

"Me, Crakow. Vait. I make more light."

"What do you do, Crakow?"

"Fix. Run school. Furnace, hair conditioning. Custodian. Chief engineer."

"Hard work, Chief?"

"Ah, everything hard. Even Crakow, eh? Hahaha. Here, you vant coffee? Some homemade bread. Sit. Zdenka make it. Wife."

"Thanks, Crakow. Thank god your kind survives. You belong upstairs. No . . . maybe this is better for you, right here."

"Cigar? Me like teachers but no talk much me. No come see Crakow in boiler room. Sometimes I up fix window or light, they say, 'Hello, Mr.

126

Crakow.' Thas nice."

"Fuck 'em, Crakow. Don't let 'em get you. Just stay down here. I'll come see you whenever I can."

"Sure, sure. You jus' come. Here's coffee. Bread, sausage there, dat locker. Soup in ice box, here hotplate. Beer too in icebox. Beer?"

"Yeah."

"Vait. I go lock door upstairs."

Hassock sitting at the table, hollering at Crakow's footsteps going up the stairs: "HOW THE HELL WILL I EVER FIND THIS PLACE AGAIN, CRAKOW? I GET LOST UPSTAIRS!"

"You jus' vait. I tell you. I fix. Easy." Crakow huffing, puffing his way back down.

"You're getting too old for this racket, Crakow. You're too heavy. Too much beer and homemade bread. Take it easy."

"Don't voory. Crakow no kill himself on this vork. Union help. See buttons? Red button, blue button?"

"Yeah."

"Thas all. Red button, vinter time heat. Blue button, spring time hair conditioning."

"What if it ain't winter or spring?"

"Is always heat or no heat. Is no other vay. Now I give you beer."

"Thanks. How do I find this place again?"

"Easy. In main circle, keep valking till you see door with red knob. Is boiler room. Easy. Open, come down."

"What if it's locked?"

"Then I drink the beer! No, no. Knock tvice, like so . . . rap! rap! I come."

"Crakow, do me a favor. Would you go up those stairs again and find my box in the office? It's somewhere near yours. Here, I'll write it out: H-a-s-s-o-c-k. Bring me whatever the hell's in there."

"Sure, sure. Hassock, huh? Bohemian in old neighborhood name, Husak. Mean 'goose' hahaha."

"That's close enough."

Hassock downing his beer. Going to the box for another. Waiting, waiting for Crakow to return with the news. He picks up a Polish newspaper and falls instantly in love with the look of the language. I wish the hell I had learned to speak this shit, he says. Thinking of the old man, the old lady, Spira, so much to learn in one lifetime. The door opening above. Crakow pounding his way down.

"Lots, lots mail. Fallin' even on floor."

Bulletins, announcements, memos, memos, memos, FROM THE

DESK OF (pink) Reckelson, (blue) Meeks, (white) Scutters . . . "Why no homework?" . . . "Why no grades?" . . . "Mrs. Ashbridge would like you to return her call" . . .

"Here, Crakow, throw all this shit in the furnace. Here's what I'm looking for:

Hassock,

I say Yes to the man with balls.
Meet me in the teachers' parking lot after school.

Green-eyes
P.S. The red Ford with the broken back window.

"Well, Crakow, it's back to work. What's the time?"

"Es 2 o'clock. Plenty time. Crakow get more beer. I guess new man no come today."

"How big a staff you got?"

"Don' know. Me never see all dem. I vork days alone. Dey jus' come night, open closets, take brooms, buckets, clean rooms and halls, then gone. Dey bunch a bozos. Main circle never clean right. Principal send memos, office dirty. So Crakow come in early every morning, no pay, clean circle, put flag up, stay sometime extra night, clean principal's office, put flag down."

"Where's the principal's office?"

"Up. Here, above. In the meedle, round the flag pole. You know principal?"

"Never met the man."

"Es beesy man. No like bothered. I go early and vacuum rug, dust desk, vipe all down with alcohol like he vants. Vipe vindows. Clean toilet."

"He's got his own crapper in there?"

"Ya, private shithouse. All tile. Nice. I keep with fresh towels, paper. Spray can."

"Where's the teacher's parking lot, Crakow? I've got an appointment there."

"Upstairs in main circle, jus' look for open doors."

"That's what I've been doing and can't seem to find my way out."

"Jus' find open doors and keep valking till you're out. Then take ray #3 all the vay to end. There, outside, teacher lot."

"Thanks, Crakow. The beers . . . everything. I'll see you again."

"Es good to see you, Hassock. Come 'gain. No forget lunchbox. Nice vone. Look like mine, es same kind."

Hassock leaping it upstairs. The door. Blinking, blind in the light of glass. Bumping into someone . . . "Are you the new man?"

"No," Hassock replies, turns . . . over . . . around . . . in . . . out! Ray #6, 5, 4, 3 . . . Hassock flashes out the door, safe in the parking lot.

"You found the car all right?"

"Easy. The only red one with a broken back window. Simple instructions. My guess is you're a hell of a good teacher. One of my clues: simple instructions. Simple and honest. Most kids screw up because the teachers themselves are so goddam confused."

"Where are we going?"

"It's your car. Drive."

"I don't feel like it."

"I don't have a license anymore. I've given up on cars. They just drive a man to self-inflicted wounds."

"But you still *know* how to drive, don't you?"

"Maybe. I'd rather sit in the back seat by the open window and watch you."

"Where to?"

"Your place?"

"How about some coffee at Howard Johnson's just off the expressway?"

"Fine. I like orange roofs. The world needs brighter colored roofs."

Hassock in a booth, staring at Green-Eyes . . .

"Don't look at me like that," she smiles and covers her face. He's thinking: I have not made love in a very long time. She is taller than me. She is warm, comforting, but most importantly — alive. He begins wooing her with wonderful stories of the old country, the new country, his own serious-comic plight of the present.

"Let's go to bed," he concludes.

"So soon? No. It's almost time for dinner. I must get going. I can't fall for a line like that."

"Where's home?"

"Down-state."

"Not another down-state farm girl?"

"Another?"

"My first wife. I mean, my ex-wife."

"Oh."

"Well, almost."

"Almost what?"

129

"A down-state farm girl. Only I went away to college. Then I sort of eloped with a man who didn't marry me after all. Worked as a cocktail waitress in New Orleans. Decided to become a teacher. Graduated from L.S.U."

"Interesting credentials."

"Fair. A solid 'B' student. No more, no less. Just an average teacher. Not like you. You, I feel, might be great."

"Might is right."

"Kirstin Wilkinson just loves you."

"That's news. We've never spoken. She's one of those quiet gazers. How did you hear that?"

"The word gets around."

"That it does. How come everybody hears about everybody else and nobody really knows anybody?"

"Isn't that always the way?"

"Yeah. What do you do in class?"

"Well, in a way I'm a technician. I'm mostly just tolerated by the kids. We don't really get to know each other in this reading racket. I'm a reading specialist, you see. I see the kids a few times a week. I give them their little reading machines, their reading records, and then it's all pretty much independent study. I'm really an English major, but I am qualified in reading as well. The school decided they needed a reading specialist, I needed to keep my job, so that's what I am. End of sad story."

"How the hell could you let them do that to you?"

"I'm really not that sharp in grammar or literature anyway. I don't read enough. I don't know enough. And maybe I'm really afraid of a whole class full of kids who may know more than I do. For crissake, Hassock, I've never even read *The Scarlet Letter!*"

"Great book. You don't know what you missed. All about this witchy chick who gets knocked up by her own minister. And everybody feels guilty as hell. Haven't I heard that some place before?"

"Tell me some good books to read."

"I will, I will. Let me sleep on it. I'll bring you some. Stick with me, kid. You have nothing to lose but your reading machines. I'll teach you everything."

"Well, not everything."

"Yes, not everything."

Monday morning is Monday morning is Monday morning forever and ever, Amen. Monday morning, Hassock has set out to destroy the day. Monday mornings require too much of people. They dictate, delineate, depress. Sunday is no help either. But Monday calls for a new leaf. Things to be done. Like the *Weekly Bulletin,* to be read every Monday in every English class so everyone will know what is expected of them the rest of the week. All in black and white. On occasion — joyous celebrations like Christmas and Homecoming — colored paper perhaps. But still black and white.

"Read it, Jack. Tell us the news for Monday, the good word for the week."

MEETINGS: Tuesday
Boy's Bowling Club—All boys interested in bowling report to room 255, ray #3 after school.
Camera Club — Are you interested in photography? You don't need a camera to join our club. Just an interest. 3:10, room 106, #2.
Wednesday
Home Economics Club — Will meet in room 122 at 3:05, ray #6. Officers will be elected and plans for Homecoming will be discussed. Anyone interested in running for vice-president, president, secretary, or historian should talk to Miss Rassis before noon tomorrow.

Thursday
War Club — Anyone who likes to play war games please meet in room 108, ray #4 at 3:15. Bring cards, games, books, what have you. We need a sponsor.

ANNOUNCEMENTS:

Juniors — Sample class rings are on display on the enclosed bulletin board behind the glass case in the main circle. Orders for the rings must be placed by next Tuesday. Get yours NOW!

Driver Education Books — Students

who wish to sell "Sportsman-like Driving" may do so today at the bookstore.

Locker Reminder — Each pupil has been assigned a locker. Some people were assigned to "double-up." The locker is a convenience for you and a help in providing for your personal property provided that you use it correctly. Proper care of your locker includes: Keeping it locked when not in use, keeping your property locked in your own locker, and keeping the inside and outside of your locker clean. It is the wise student who does not give other students their combination.

Smoking Regulations — In the interest of improving the status of the entire student body and abiding by the State Law in cooperation with the local law enforcement officers, pupils are asked not to smoke anytime within sight of the school nor at anytime of school sponsored activities — at home or away. (Better yet, don't smoke period!) Any student who is apprehended will be subject to a three-day suspension and will be reported to the local law enforcement agency. Any student who carries smoking materials into the school or stores them in their locker shows a lack of willingness to cooperate with the law and will be suspended for three days. Likewise, those students who smoke in cars or busses within sight of the school plant will be subject to the same suspension stated above.

Lunch — For the time of your lunch at any given day, see "Lunch Schedules" posted on the bulletin board in the Main Circle.

Proper Dress & Grooming — All pupils are expected to present a neat appearance at all times and are urged to use good taste in their manner of dress. It is pointed out that any type of clothing or hairstyle that calls unnecessary attention to a person is not desirable. For boys, the hair should be preferably short and trim. It is recommended that the boys wear a wash slack (clean) with a belt. Sport shirts should be properly buttoned with the shirt tail IN at all times. Shoes should be a loafer type or any other type of low cut leather shoe. Western type trousers of any cut (including white) are forbidden on these premises. Likewise, boots or shoes with cleats are not to be worn. Girls, too, are expected to use common sense and good taste in their dress habits. Skirts should not creep above the knee when sitting down. All classroom teachers will please report girls wearing skirts too short to the point of distraction. (Girls, if when you kneel on the floor, your skirt does not touch, it is too short.) Teachers, counselors, deans, administrators may apply this short skirt test at their discretion.

Cafeteria — In going to the cafeteria today, and everyday, for lunch, please do not run or push. There will be time and food and room enough for all. Tomorrow, each table will elect a table captain, and he or she will list the names of the people at your table for the semester. Cleanliness and order must be maintained.

New American Flags — The new flags
this year in all the classrooms, and the
center pole, are the class gift from last
year's graduation seniors. Principal
Scutters would like you all to be reminded of this, thankful to the senior
class, and thankful to our community,
country, and God for the freedom of
education we all share in this great
land. Thank you.

"Thank you, thank you. Thank you, Jack. Thank you all. Well, we have
our information for the week. Our orders, don't we? Inspection! Front
and center all you girls. Get a move on, get a move on! Let's go, let's get up
here! I want one rank right in front of Hassock here. Come on, come on.
Okay . . . Diane, up a few steps. Joy, make room for Emma. Okay, girls,
attention please. Fellas, just sit still and mind your own business for a
minute. All right, girls, kneel! Let's have a little inspection. Emma . . .
okay. Dismissed. Gloria, about a quarter of an inch too high. Joy, you're
on report. The tops of your stockings are clearly too visible. Diane, all
right. Kirstin . . . too high. On report. Now tell me, girls, while you're still
kneeling before me, how do you feel?"

"Embarrassed" . . . "Dumb" . . .

"Good. Enough. Your lesson for today: Don't always follow orders.
Especially when they demean you or others. Go on back to your desks.
I'm sorry."

"The Pledge of Allegiance, Hassock," says Jack.

"You caught me at a bad time. Listen, I think teaching, learning, has
something to do with lessening the load. Feeling light. Making it all a little
more simple. That's one of the things we're going to try and do. The past
can be a hell of a burden. You can't always move forward with adventure
if you're going to continue lugging the past on your back and add to it.
Jack, I don't have time for the Pledge. Or maybe there's something else I
want to explore. Let me teach, huh? Give me the space. We're all Americans here, aren't we? We love this country. I want to get beyond patriot-
ism. There are a hell of a lot of flags out there in the world. Maybe one is a
better way. Or none. Let's give ourselves more room. I don't care to waste
any more time on the weekly bulletin either. It's posted in the main circle.
All of us can read. So let's leave it there. Shedding, folks. That's what
we're doing. Getting light."

"Mr. Hassock?"

"Hassock, Karl, Hassock."

"Hassock, all of this is contrary to school policy. If they find out, you'll be fired. They fired my history teacher last year. The American Legion came and everything. They accused him of teaching socialism because of a unit on Norman Thomas. They said he was a Communist because of the books he assigned and the things he said in class."

"Yeah, I had a teacher like that once too. He organized the teachers into a union in my high school. They called him a Commie too and gave him nothing but hell. He was one of the best teachers I ever had. Accept nobody else's answers. There's a lot of bullshit you have to deal with. There's a lot of it, I've discovered, right here in this school."

"You know what's going to happen to you, Hassock," says Jack.

"Maybe. That reminds me. Somebody's talking in here. My box runneth over with bad news. Who's been squealing to Scutters?"

"Hassock, I mentioned to my father how easy English was now that I have you. He may have called the school."

"Thanks, Nick. Jack?"

"I know my parents called for certain. They asked for a conference with Mr. Scutters and my counselor. It's about grades. You seem to be a good guy and everything, but we haven't had any tests or any homework so far. And we're all sort of lost."

"Karl?"

"Grades are the main thing, Hassock. We really need them to get into good colleges, and nobody understands just what you're trying to do. I've had teachers before who moan about how they hate to give grades, but in the end they do. They all do. They *have* to."

"Christ, you people scare the hell out of me. Grades. What have I been trying to get at with you people for the past few weeks? Are we still on square one? What do you expect to do with the rest of your lives? How the hell do you expect to survive? By grades? By the right colleges? By degrees? You want to grow up and become assholes like this whole administration? Do you know what counselors are? Stunted human beings. Failed teachers. They think the secret to life is better living through more testing. They're more interested in numbers and bell curves than you. And if they don't know who they are, how the hell do they have the nerve to tell you what you are according to numbers, and what you ought to become? You want grades? You're worried about grades? And homework? And life beyond Highland High? Okay. Let's see just how honest you are with yourselves. Let's shed something else. A deal, now. Hassock's new deal. Everybody in? A pact, if you will. And for nobody's listening pleasure outside this classroom. I want honesty, sincerity, and a leap toward humanity! Here's the deal, and I've got to see all nine hands up, or we're

135

in real trouble — which probably means the return of Reckelson and *Grammatical Constructions for Life.* And that's no threat, just the truth. You all have 'A's' in this course from this moment on. Each marking period and the final grade. All homework, whether I assign any or not, 'A' work. So breath comfortably. You're class records are guaranteed."

"I don't get it," says Marvin. "It sounds unfair. What do we tell our parents?"

"It's your education, not theirs. Trust me, for now, with your education. We are writing in those notebooks, we're talking, we'll be reading, the learning is already beginning. I'm baking, you know? Hassock's cooking! You'll see, maybe someday, the results. But no tests. No grades or old fashioned homework. Okay now, give me a show of hands: 1 . . . 2 . . . 3 . . . 4 . . . 5 . . . 6 . . . 7 . . . 8 . . . What's wrong, Gloria?"

"I don't know. I don't think this is right. I'm confused. I've never held anything back from my parents."

"Just once, Gloria. Give me a chance. Let me try . . . thanks. Thanks, Gloria, thanks. We're all in. I feel good. You guys are the best thing to happen to me in a long time. I thank the whole small bunch of you. Now, for tomorrow, bring your copies of *Adventures in American Literature.* I've already asked you to start reading, on the outside, some Steinbeck, Huxley, and Camus. We'll begin now, somewhere, with the required text. Oh, one more thing. I keep forgetting. Don't ever, all of you, sit in front of me in two straight rows again. Sit wherever you damn well please. All right. It's time for me to stop sounding like a teacher. I hate myself now. Because that, my friends, all that we've been through so far, was pure explication. I am almost certain of that. Don't force me into it again. Nothing of any great value (for your own enlightenment) ever comes from explication, *de el professor! Verdad?* I am almost certain of that. See you tomorrow. Wait till the bell rings. Jack, cover for me. Hassock doth protest too much. His mouth is dry. Enough. I'll make an early exit out the back door."

"So long, Hassock." "Bye." "So long." "See you tomorrow, Mr. Hassock."

Out the back door, lunchbox swinging down the hill up the hill into the cloverleaf where the blue bus lies hissing at Hassock. Hassock hisses back. Alone in a rear seat, he opens his box, pours a cup of coffee, and contemplates anew *The Green-Eyed Nympho:* "You have a very beautiful body, my dear," he whispered in an emotion choked voice. "Come and stand over here where I can see you better."

"Hey, who is that woman with the wrinkled head always peeking in the lounge at this time of the morning?"

"Miss Sluer," says Clay. "Miss Josie J. Sluer. 63 years old, teacher of advanced classes in English literature, official busybody, reporter, and headcount artist. She wants to be sure we're all in here drinking coffee, smoking, lounging, instead of grading papers. That is her job. That is her way of life. Every English department has a Sluer. It's a symbiotic arrangement."

"I think she's been spying on my class too. I'm sure I saw that gray wooly head gathering dust around my door."

"Very likely," says Green-eyes. "She's always walking past my room, shaking her head if she sees me sitting down. Once she even stepped right into my room and told a student to be quiet. Right in front of me!"

"What she needs she no longer remembers, or ever knew. Right, Clay?"

"Precisely, Hassock. I'm gonna get me one a them flannel shirts you wear sometime."

"What the hell kind of accent you got, Clay?"

"He's a Hoosier," says Elsie.

"You still here? I thought you were meditating on my pronunciation or something?"

"You are not worth it, Hassock. And listen, you don't scare me. You bad actors are a dime a dozen. You don't have the language to insult me. You know what the studies say about people who must depend upon profanity to express themselves, don't you? Limited vocabulary. I don't even sympathize with you, Hassock."

"Say, how are you on reading hand signals? Remember this one, Clay? Bam! Up goes the right arm? Pronounce this, Elsie. What do the studies say about people with vocabularies so limited they must resort to archaic Italian gestures of the hand?"

"Very funny, Hassock. Rude. Crude. Childish mentality."

"You know, Elsie, I think you're beginning to understand me. It could be love."

"Don't count on it."

"So you're a fucking Hoosier, Clay! What the hell do you teach, anyway?"

"Nothing. I have four 'disadvantaged' classes. One of them black. I have four dummy classes because I am a dummy, hahahaha."

"And what does a dummy teach in dummy English?"

"Dummy literature, dummy grammar. The difference between a period and a question mark."

"I wonder about that myself."

"I use a watered-down version of the *Adventures* series called, *Adventures in Space.*"

"Perfect. I mean, yeah, of course. What about the blacks. What do you do with them? I've never seen one around here by the way. What's in the English program for them?"

"Space. The same thing."

"Are you getting anywhere?"

"Nope. I've taught dummy classes for 10 years, and I've never gotten anywhere because there is no way to go. I am doing my job. And the school is pleased, the parents seemed pleased, and I'm pleased. Well, pleased . . . You know. The kids show up every day. They behave. They will graduate with everyone else. Most of them will receive 'certificates' instead of diplomas, and go out into the world where everything is hunky-dory."

"Clay, you're a good teacher?"

"No, I am a very bad teacher. But I *know* I am very bad. And I don't care. False . . . I do care. But I make good money. I am a good man. And I am happy as a little green apple.

"You can't be that fucking pleased with yourself, Clay. Teach them something, for crissake! Or be something! It's bullshit, what you're doing. I was a dummy English kid myself. The counselors, you know. The tests put me there. I want a whole class full of dark dummies sometime. I want to try that."

"What would you try?"

"I don't know. Black, maybe. Everything black. Beginning with 'Little Black Sambo'."

"We talk about George Washington Carver. And all he did for the little peanut."

"Up Carver. I'm talking about 'Little Black Sambo.' Maybe some Negro songs and spirituals. I love that music. On Sunday nights in bed I like to turn the radio dial all the way to the end and just listen to those black gospel preachers shout and sing. Why don't you tape one of those guys sometime? Bring it to class. Talk about it. And talk about Wright and Baldwin. Hughes, Langston Hughes and Gwendolyn Brooks. She wrote a beautiful little novel, *Maud Martha,* and nobody even knows about it. I may teach it myself for the girls' sake. It's about growing up and becoming a woman. There's enough there for us all."

"What do you know about women, Hassock?"

"Elsie, allow me to show you sometime."

"That's what I thought."

"Green-eyes, tell your friend, Elsie, how I feel about women. How I care."

"Hassock is harmless. He took me out once and sat in the back seat while I drove. He is a gentle man."

"See! What did I tell you, Elsie?"

"There she goes again," says Clay.

"Who?"

"Sluer. She's doing a headcount to make sure we're all here. Now comes Reckelson."

"Hello, gang. How's everybody doing today? Collection time again. Missed most of you the last time. Fifty cents, please, will keep the coffee pot boiling for another week."

"How much of a cut do you get from the kitty?" asks Clay. "You must collect twenty or thirty bucks a week. The whole department don't drink that much coffee."

" 'Doesn't.' Whatever is left over goes in the department fund. You know that, Mike."

"What's the department fund?" asks Hassock.

"We build up this little departmental fund for special emergencies — sickness, death, things like that. A suitable plant or floral piece. A nice policy. Ah, thank you Miss Skyes, Miss Ellsworth, Mike. And Hassock?"

"I'm a part-timer. I bring my own coffee."

"What about the department fund?"

"I'll tell you what, Reckelson. When I die, just skip it. I'll understand."

"I'm sorry you feel that way. There goes the bell. I'll see you people."

"Well, Green-eyes, what do you say you and me beer it up this week sometime, and I give you another chance to show you how I feel about women?" Maybe Elsie'd like to join us and make it an orgy?"

"Sorry, but I'll have to disappoint you," says Miss Ellsworth. "I'm not your kind."

"There's no adventure in you, Elsie."

"Sure," says Green-eyes. "When? Where?"

"You know the area better than I do."

"Well, maybe the Nook. About a mile west of here."

"Okay if I bum a ride from you? Today? Tomorrow?"

"Anytime."

Hassock stepping lively to his class. Kids passing, pushing, shoving. The customary first-bell fever in the halls. A hand grabs Hassock — a teacher: "Are you the new man? My window won't open in room 121. Can you fix it?" "Sorry, wrong man. See Crakow." Hassock backing into the doorway of his own room. Into the arms of Reckelson.

"Wear a white shirt, Hassock, for crissake," he says. "And another thing, watch the romance, if you know what I mean."

"No."

"Carol Skyes."

"Romance? It's barely begun."

"Keep it outside the school walls. Tongues will wag."

"You mean Scout Sluer?"

"Why aren't these kids in their assigned seats?"

"Who's to say where anyone should sit?"

"Hassock, you're dealing in danger. Meeks, by the way, definitely wants to see you sometime. The proper procedure is for you to invite him to sit in on one of your class sessions. That's the way we do things here: invitation only. He's anxious to meet you. Send him a note. Today! Missed you at the last full faculty meeting."

"I wasn't invited. I'm just a part-timer here, you know."

"You were invited. Everybody was. Didn't you see the note in your box?"

"I've been having problems with that box."

"Department meeting next week. I'm inviting you, personally. Don't forget. And, oh, be careful with that guy, Clay. I think he's a little cracked. My only bad move in recruiting for the English Department so far. I may have goofed. He was supposed to be an expert with disadvantaged kids. That's why I hired him. In 10 years, that's all he's ever taught. Well, now I find out he's been fired from every school he's ever taught in. I can't understand why his records never revealed that. I'll probably end up firing him myself. He just sits with them. Doesn't teach them how to read or spell or write."

"Why don't you give him some advantaged kids for a change?"

"Are you kidding? What the hell would he do with them?"

"Probably teach them a hell of a lot."

"I can't. He's our disadvantaged teacher. I budgeted for him."

"If he's disadvantaged, what am I?"

"A character. Get to work. And get those kids in their proper seats."

"Lock the door, Marvin. Let's everybody take a look at *Adventures in American Literature* and see what's to be done with it. Turn to the section on the colonial period and tear out everything by Taylor, and Sarah-baby-Knight. Then . . ."

"Hassock?"

"Emma?"

"Are you kidding?"

"No."

"Literally 'tear out' these pages?"

"Literally, figuratively, tear out all those goddam pages that are boring as hell, speak no adventure, and have nothing to do with who we are and what we might become. Yes. Rip out Sarah Baby, Johnny Edwards, William the Byrd. Franklin, Henry, Paine, Jefferson, etc. Suit yourself. They're all right — but they're all history. We're looking for literature. American, at the moment. Ah ... Washington Irving ... out. No hard feelings. Ditto Bryant, Whittier, Poe. You had Poe up to your ears in grade school, didn't you? 'The Raven,' 'The Bells,' and all that bull . . ."

"I like the story about the guy that gets bricked into a wall," says Karl.

"That's what I mean. 8th grade horror movie stuff. Let's pass Poe. Hawthorne too."

"What about *The Scarlet Letter?*" asks Gloria. "It's on the junior reading list. It's one of my mother's favorites."

"I'm not saying you can't read it. Read what you want. We'll talk about it. Sooner or later we'll try to touch it all. I just don't happen to feel Hawthorne's really American literature either. Too damn English. Purely personal. Maybe he belongs in Josie Sluer's English Lit. course. The main thing, he's a drag for people your age. *Moby Dick,* we'll keep. *Moby Dick*, or whatever part of him that they chose to include in this anthology, we'll save for sometime later. He might come in handy."

"How about poetry, Hassock?"

"How about it? I love it. Yes, of course, we'll do something with it. And listen, back in that early section, save 'The Painted History of the Delware Indians.' I'd like us to look into that too. Okay, where are we? Emerson, keep. Thoreau, keep. Longfellow ... oh, I don't know. Maybe. Keep the entire 'Western Movement' section. As for Twain, let's begin there. I want everyone to read *Huck Finn.* The complete novel. Get a copy somewhere. Keep the whole modern section too. There's an interesting book review in there about a novel on bullfighting. Anybody here ever see a bullfight?"

"They're illegal in this country, Hassock."

"I *know* that, for crissake! There's a restriction on dying for the hell of it in the States. Okay then, that's it. That's your new adventure book. Always subject to change. And very subject to be beefed up at anytime with anything the teacher feels like using. As for composition, we'll center it all around literature. Did I forget anything?"

"What about spelling?" asks Jack.

"Hmmmmm. Spelling. You mean the 100 Most Misspelled Words?

Just plan old everyday spelling, huh? I'll tell you what. You give me a test. Here, I'll go to the blackboard, I mean the greenboard, and you start calling out some words . . . "

"Constitution . . . "

"Let's see . . . c o n s t a t u t i o n . . . no . . . another one."

"Proceed . . . "

"p r o c e d e"

"Occasion . . . "

"o c a s s i o n"

"Those are all wrong, Hassock," says Emma.

"How do you know? Look them up. Does everybody have a dictionary? From now on, bring a pocket dictionary with you to class at all times. That's it. Why don't you begin reading some Mark Twain till the bell rings."

"I see you found my car again," says Green-eyes.

"What do you do about this open back window in the snow and rain?"

"I let the back seat fill up with it."

"Keep talking, Green-eyes. I'm falling in love with you."

"I asked Clay to join us. Do you mind?"

"Clay, come on. Sit in the back here with me."

"Oh, come on you guys. How the hell is that going to look, me driving two grown men around in the back seat? Clay, here. You drive."

"Whatever you say, just as long as I get me some beer 'cause I am thirsty."

"Drive, Clay. Green-eyes and me will make love in the back seat. It's been years."

"Green-eyes will sit in front, thank you."

"I think you been hanging around too much with Elsie. She's a bad influence on you."

Pulling up to the Nook. Hassock jumps out the back window, racing to hold the door for Clay, bowing to Green-eyes, then leading them inside to a corner table.

"Beer!" yells Clay. "With a little helper on the side."

"Just a helper for me," yells Hassock. "Make that two helpers. Say, who the hell are we yelling at anyway? I can't see a soul in the dark."

"The bartender," says Clay. "That's who's in the dark. He's the lost soul. The tavern — where kindred spirits are joined together. Over there in the darkness is the bar. And behind it, always a bartender, keeper of the spirits. And today, brothers and sisters, the lesson is thirst. And so, there *will* be light."

142

"Imagine that! A man after my own words! Crissake, Clay, you're really something."

"I'm a great something."

"What do you read?"

"Nothing. Once upon a time I read Melville. I got me a Master's in *Moby Dick*. For five summers I chased the white whale until he finally surfaced and sounded me to a funny farm in southern Indiana. There I sat, rusty harpoon in hand, for many a month by a sea which was all corn and tiny green apples. My Master's in *Moby* came through the mails. Call me Ishmael."

"I think we should all change our names as we outgrow them and seek different selves. And maybe end up anonymous," says Hassock.

"I like that, Hassock. But 'Green-eyes' was not a choice of mine."

"You'll learn, my love. But, Clay, what's a man with a Master's in *Moby* doing teaching in a sea of 'disadvantaged'?"

"That's where I found myself when I was hired. Empathy or something, I guess. I've never been known to make waves."

Green-eyes taking hold of Clay's arm in a loving way.

"How come I thought you were my woman?" asks Hassock.

"Oh, it may be I am. And Clay's. There's enough to go around."

"Hold me too, Green-eyes, the way you hold Clay."

"What's your story, Hassock?" mumbles Clay.

"Oh, it's not very interesting. Rather confusing, to tell you the truth. At times I think I'm the main character. Then I meet men like you, women like this, and I know I still amount to nothing, and the story may never end."

"Married?"

"That's another story with a bad ending."

"Who was she? What was she like, Hassock?" asks Green-eyes.

"Foolish questions, my love. I expect you can do better than that. What you really want to know, is how she compares to you. Not as beautiful . . . good enough in bed for the time. She will no doubt make a great mother someday. Like most first marriages, it's something you have to work through each other. And sometimes you must work your way right out."

"So what happened?" asks Clay.

"Goddam it, man, how the hell do you expect me to answer that? You and your fucking man/whale stories. What the hell do you know about man/woman tales?"

"I'm married. How's that for a plot?"

"I don't give a shit. That's your life, not mine."

143

"Hassock doesn't like happy endings, Clay."

"Kiss my ass, Green-eyes. What the hell do you know anyway? You had the hots for one man, ran off with him, and then got screwed all the way around. You became a cocktail waitress, found out it was too good to be true, so you got good old Downstate Illinois Religion again, decided to straighten out and fly right and become a teacher — a humanitarian gesture. Home safe. Now you find yourself teaching reading like a science and wonder why you can't relate to kids. Happy horseshit ending, eh?"

"Hassock, you must be drunk. Don't talk to me like that."

"Yeah, I'm drunk and I'm depressed and I'm elated. I don't need to rely on this stuff anymore like Clay over there. Or you. Let's talk about those kids. Those kids we're supposed to be teaching. Well, what the hell are we teaching? What are you offering them, Clay, that will make them any better than you?"

"Not a goddam thing. I wasn't hired for that. And if you don't shut your goddam mouth, you're gonna have trouble talking."

"Fuck you, Clay. Go play with your whale."

"Hassock, stop it! Do you want to go now? Should we leave?"

"No, no. I'm sorry. I'm just feeling my way out loud. Clay knows about that, right Clay? Tell me what you discovered about yourself on that funny farm."

"Nothing. Except I'm going to die. And that scares the hell out of me."

"No real breakthrough, buddy. I've been there before. Bang! you're dead. Now what?"

"There's love," says Green-eyes.

"You and your goddam Class B movie dialogue. How much of that have you really given this poor bastard? Enough to keep him alive?"

"He's never asked."

"Oh, shit, baby. Look at me! I'm crying. Over what? Spilt milk? You? Me? Clay?"

"Hassock, you keep this up and you're gonna end up in a straight-jacket," says Clay.

"Okay, white-jacket. Let's drink. Let's smoke. Green-eyes, do you mind if I put my hand on your leg? Let's love. These kids of mine...only nine of them, but they're all dead. Do you know that?"

"Hassock," she whispers, "quit feeling sorry for them and us and everything. It's not your fault."

"Dead, Clay. I'm surrounded by death these days. Except for Crakow. Do you know him? That greenhorn in the basement? I was down there the other day and we ate his old lady's blood soup together. You go talk to Crakow. He's the only one alive in the whole fucking school."

"So, what are you teaching them?" mumbles Clay. "What's the answer?"

"I don't know, I don't know. Just watch me, that's all. For the anti-climax I may do myself in. But goddam it, I will not sacrifice those kids to all the bullshit that's made us such sad creatures."

"Hassock, I'm sorry, but I find it difficult to follow you any more," she says. "One more drink, yes? Then I'll take you home with me."

"Now that's the beginning of a whole new story I'd like to be a part of. Clay, to you. Trust me, us, all of it."

"Some specifics," says Clay. "Just what are you teaching now?"

"*Adventures in American Literature.* What else? We're done with grammar and spelling for the year, also *The Scarlet Letter,* the whole colonial period. I've carved out a nice block of time to just explore the territory. At the moment, we're about to wind up *The Adventures of Huckleberry Finn,* although we haven't discussed it yet. After Huck maybe some poetry. I try to take my movement from them. It depends on what kind of ideas we get into, which may lead us into still other books and writers for more questions and answers. Okay, Green-eyes."

"You were terrible, Hassock, just terrible the way you attacked Clay. And me. Why do you do this with everybody? What do you love?"

"Nice apartment. How can you stand living alone. That's funny. I meant 'living.' Why don't you put some paintings on the wall? I'll give you one of my watercolors sometime."

"Clay is a very sensitive man. You could have destroyed him. You can't do that to him again. He's already gone under once and barely survived. I hate to think what he's feeling this very moment, or what the scene holds when he steps into it."

"Green-eyes, please. You said yourself it's nobody's fault. Come to bed. I want to see and hold you in the flesh. God, it's been so long."

"Oh, Hassock, I'm afraid to start anything serious with you. Let's not call it love, huh. Just . . . "

"Fucking?"

"Something like that."

"Hunger? Thirst? Lust?"

"Yeah. All of the above. Don't say anymore."

"Now you're talking my kind of language — silence. I'll just watch you undress, and then we'll communicate in ways most old and telling."

"Oh, Hassock, you are beyond me."

"Yes."

"Marvin?"

"Hassock, there's somebody looking through the window near the door."

"That's just Scout Sluer. Let's all give her the old finger gesture. See! She's gone. Now, has everyone finished reading *Huck Finn?* Let's talk about the middle and the end. That's all that interests me. I don't understand that Nigger Jim business, do you, Kirstin?"

"No."

"What do you mean, no? What don't you understand?"

"What he's supposed to be and everything."

"What do you mean, what he's supposed to be? He's a nigger, a runaway slave, isn't he? What the hell else is there? Yeah, Jack?"

"As a runaway slave, Jim is an outlaw . . . "

"What about Huck?"

"Well, I guess Huck is too in a way."

"What do you mean, in a way?"

"Because he ran away from home and everything, and ah . . . "

"Karl?"

"Huck is harboring a criminal so he's just as guilty as Jim."

"Good. I like that. It's against the law to keep a criminal from the law, isn't it?"

"Yes."

"But what is the crime? What is the question, Emma?"

"The crime is that both Huck and Jim are guilty of going against the majority."

"Majority? What majority? What the hell are you talking about. I've got two people here, that's all!"

"Please, Hassock. You don't have to shout at me. I'm talking about the majority in a democracy. The majority makes the laws, and therefore everyone is expected to obey. Otherwise we have anarchy. Both Huck and Jim are in the minority. And they are both wrong."

"Jesus. You must have some mighty fine history teachers around here."

"Emma's right," says Jack.

"But are the laws always right? Was slavery right? Is it democratic to keep a human being in bondage? Aren't laws designed to be broken when they are not fair? Marvin?"

"It was right and lawful at that time, I guess. That's what Jack means. Today, of course, it should be different. But it probably isn't."

"Good going, Marvin. Take the rest of the day off with pay."

"Still, Hassock, the problem is an individual one, isn't it? I mean, it's Huck who decides to cover up for Jim. And it's Huck who . . . oh, I don't know what I mean. I can't say it."

"That's fine, Gloria. It's okay. Think about it some more. You see, there are plenty of things to think about in the story. It just may be the single masterpiece in American literature. No one was saying these things about us till Twain came along. Follow up on him sometime and read what he had to say about God. You don't have to *believe* it. But read it. Especially you Youth for Christ people. How the hell can you be only 16 years old and pledge your lives, your feelings to God, when you haven't yet learned all the great feelings the Devil has in store for you? Anyway, read the real Twain sometime. Read *1601*. I'm sure it isn't in the school library, but I'll get you a copy if you like. Where is the school library, anyway?"

"On the other side of the main circle. Next to Health."

"No wonder I've never found it. What about the ending? How does the story end? Not 'how?' Why? Diane? Don't go shrugging your shoulders at me. That's no answer. Damn it, Diane, you haven't said a word all the weeks I've been here. What the hell's with you anyway? All right, get all red and embarrassed and everything. But damn it, you better start saying something soon, or I'll transfer your arse right out of here into somebody else's class. Joy?"

"It ends with Huck thinking about running away again."

"That was not the question. Why? I asked. Why? Nick?"

"He's a wild kid, that's all. He can't sit still. I mean, why should be sit around there and do nothing and let people tell him what to do all the time? He wants to move out."

"Yeah. Good. Right. Huck's the kind of person who just has to keep moving? Anything wrong with that? Jack?"

"But he just can't continue running away from things he doesn't like. He has to settle down eventually."

"A rolling stone gathers no moss, right Jack? Crissake, you must be 60 years old, Jack."

"Well, Hassock . . . "

"That's right, shout! Get angry at me. Holler like you got a pair! What is it!"

"All right! So he runs away again! He doesn't want to be civilized. But he *has* to be! Sooner or later he has to stop running!"

"And then what, Jack? And then what? Tell me, Jack, what then? WHAT? DO YOU HEAR ME, JACK? WHAT HAPPENS WHEN A MAN STOP RUNNING?"

147

"He . . . dies."

"Thank you. You've got a hell of a mind. Use it! Now put some of this in your writing notebooks. Use all this stuff. Mull it over. Think it out on paper. Hassock has no answers. He rests his case. Anybody want a cup of coffee? I'm thirsty. I'm hungry. You all go ahead and think about Huck and everything. Think about that river. Christ, think about that river! And think about poetry. Now's the right time for poetry, I feel. Yeah . . . for tonight, try to remember everything you've been taught about poetry. And for tomorrow, forget it all. Title a page in your notebook, 'Poem.' And study the emptiness. Cover for me, Jack. Time for another early exit."

"So long, Hassock." "Bye." "Hey, Hassock! You forgot your Thermos."

"How goes the white whale today, friend?"

"Sounding, Hassock. Sounding."

"You people never make any sense," chimes Elsie. "I can't understand you."

"That's because you're a speech teacher. Look, Clay. I brought you something. Peace offering. Right here in my magic lunchbox. Close your eyes."

"Hassock! A flannel shirt just like yours?"

"Wear it in good faith, friend."

"Jesus, thank you, Hassock."

"You don't have to wear it here. Wear it around the house, or when you're out drinking. Wear it whenever you feel good. You might get in trouble wearing it around school since you're a full-timer. They got this dress-code you know. You could be tried and sentenced by the student council. A week of hard labor with Elsie here or something. Me, they don't touch. Nobody even knows I'm here. Hell, I still haven't met Meeks!"

"You will, dear, you will," sings Green-eyes.

"Not a chance. Reckelson says it's by invitation only. And I'm just never going to invite that soft-shoed bastard to my class."

"How do you know he's a bastard?" says Elsie. "I mean, Hassock, you're really paranoid or something. Miss Sluer is after you. Principal Scutters is after you. You don't trust Reckelson, or even your own students, for that matter. And now Mr. Meeks, whom you have never even met, is a bastard. The suffering hero, Hassock. Everybody's persecuting him. What temerity!"

"Don't use such big words in front of disadvantaged teachers. Elsie, you and I must go out sometime. Here, here's my address. Pick me up. And don't ever use 'whom' in my presence again."

"A date? That's a laugh. We have nothing in common. We hate each other."

"Exactly. Oh, no. Not Reckelson again! He's beginning to spoil my breakfast."

"Can I see you for a minute, Hassock?"

"Is my name 'Hassock?' Can I escape? Back to the corner, folks. Pray for me now while I'm gone."

"Something's come up that could be serious, Hassock. A few things, as a matter of fact. Number one, why aren't you shaving? You look like hell."

"It's me under here. I mean, the me that used to be me. What's the matter with a mustache? My father used to wear one. Once upon a time he was Magyar. We're a hairy bunch of bastards from way back."

"It looks terrible, Hassock. It's just not clean. I'd shave it off if I were you. And certainly get rid of it before you see Meeks. Have you invited him yet?"

"You know the answer to that. Actually, though, I'm working on a rough draft of the invitation. It begins like this: Dear Meeks, Dance your sweet ass right past my room."

"That'll get you far."

"Maybe the next dance?"

"Let's get down to business."

"Which is foreshading for: Hassock, you're in trouble again."

"I think it's safe to say that this is just between you and me. The memos have stopped coming from Meeks and Scutters, so that's just fine. Thank you. But now someone from your class is writing me notes concerning what's going on in that room."

"No big mystery. Probably Jack Smith. He's a fucking little fascist, I fear. He'll fit in real fine in this school system someday."

"I don't know who it is, and I don't care. What the hell's going on, Hassock? No weekly bulletin, no Pledge of Allegiance, no spelling, no grammar. Tearing up the textbook! Eating in class. Swearing. Leaving before the bell. Hassock, you must be suicidal. You'll never last the year this way. Don't even think about coming back next year. I couldn't possibly hire you. Not unless you turn over a new leaf . . . "

"Don't be so fucking trite."

"Stop all this nonsense and get down to some good, hard teaching. Remember, 'Experience keeps a dear school, but a fool will learn in no other'."

"And, 'A small leak will sink a great ship.' And, 'One today is worth two tomorrows.' And, 'Glass, china, and reputation are easily cracked and never well-mended.' And, 'Three may keep a secret if two of them are dead'!"

"Hassock, calm down . . . "

"'TIS HARD FOR AN EMPTY BAG TO STAND UPRIGHT!' 'A PLOWMAN ON HIS LEGS IS HIGHER THAN A GENTLEMAN ON HIS KNEES!' 'WHEN THE WELL'S DRY, WE KNOW THE WORTH OF WATER'!"

"Hassock, sit down."

"'A TRULY GREAT MAN WILL NEITHER TRAMPLE ON A WORM NOR SNEAK TO AN EMPEROR'!"

"SIT DOWN, HASSOCK!"

"'FISH AND VISITORS SMELL IN THREE DAYS! FUCK YOU, POOR RICHARD RECKELSON!"

"Have you people ever been in love? That's what poetry is all about. Much of it, anyway. In love? Love? Why such dumb stares? Crissake, don't tell me it's against the law to love at your age? Marvin?"

"Ah, don't call on me."

"Do you have a girl? Isn't there somebody you go out with? Would like to go out with?"

"No one steady. I'll ask a girl to a school dance maybe. That's all."

"Joy? Joy! You're wearing someone's class ring around your neck. Tell me how you got that ring."

"It belongs to Rick Carlson on the football team. He's a senior."

"Joy, how come you never answer my question? How did you get that ring?"

"Well, what do you want me to tell you? Everything?"

"Nick, quit smiling. You too, Marvin. Yes, everything."

"We went to the Junior Prom together last year. That's when he gave it to me. He asked me to go steady."

"All right, come down. What's poetry, Joy?"

"I don't know."

"You've got a steady boyfriend. There's poetry between you, no?"

"I don't know what you mean."

"Somebody else? Poetry, anyone? Jack?"

"Poetry is a certain use of language. When you use words in a certain pattern, and rhymes, then you have poetry."

"You mean like, 'Hickory, Dickory Dock/The mouse ran up the

clock/The clock struck one and hit him in the ass' — is that poetry?"

"In a way. Except for the 'ass' part."

"Well, my ass it is. Forget about rhyme, for the time being. I don't want to hear that word. I want to talk about poetry. I don't suppose you have a steady girl, Jack?"

"I told you once before, no."

"Has anything really exciting ever happened to you?"

"Sure. Lots of things."

"Like?"

"I got accepted in Honors Physics this year."

"Shit. You people are backing me against the wall again. Take out some paper. For tomorrow or the next day or whenever the hell I feel like talking about poetry again, you better have something poetic on that paper. You better tell me in plain old fashioned prose about things that happened to you. Experiences that made you feel happy, overjoyed, sad, depressed, confused, loving, sexy, you name it. Then we'll see what poetry's all about. Then we'll see what poets you are. Hands? Emma?"

"I don't understand what you mean. What kind of experiences? Just anything?"

"What-do-I-mean? What-do-I-mean? What-do-I-mean? If I told you I don't know what I mean, would that mean anything? Come here, Emma. Turn around and face the class. Smile, Here, SLAP! How does that feel across the face? How do you feel? How do you think I feel? Go ahead, cry. But tell me how you feel, Emma. I'll see you guys. Thank you, Emma."

"Old man, how about some two-handed pinochle?"

"Auuugh . . ."

"You want another whiskey? Okay. One more glass. Me too. You happy? Me, not so good. I got a woman coming to pick me up tonight. Woman, ha! A teacher. A Miss Ellsworth. A real bitch. The kind of woman you would probably kick the hell out of. Why did you do that to the old lady all the time? Tell me? She spent her whole goddam life looking after you, and you treated her like crap! Is that what they taught you in the old country? Who the hell did you think you were anyway? Some Hungarian King? What did you ever do for her? You'd say you were going to wash the windows, and she'd get the water ready for you, get the ladder out of the basement, stand there in the windy gangway and hold the ladder for you so you wouldn't fall. Or you'd shovel snow, but she'd have to find the shovel for you. You did the job, but she made all the preparations, did all the cleaning-up afterwards. You took her to church every Sunday. Very noble, old man. You never bought her a goddam thing. Not

151

one gift! Never took her anywhere she might want to go. Just work every day, and she'd be up hours before you, packing a lunch in the dark, making breakfast. After work, she would still be at the stove cooking. How the hell do you call that love? How did the two of you make love? Why? Ah, old man, what a fucking life we Magyars must live. I saw your Yugoslavia, you know. Sarajevo is still the same. And all the Bogomils are buried. The bulls, old man, the bulls. They are all around us, staring in every wall. Drink. Here. Now hold those fucking cards straight. I can see your hand, and I won't let you lose."

"Come in a minute, Elsie. No, this way through the gangway, down the back stairs."

"Why don't you cut the lawn?"

"Nobody lives here anymore. Anyway, I like the prairie effect. Tall grass, weeds, flowers poking through where they can. I'm down here in the front of the basement. Watch your step."

"You should water the plants. They seem to be dying of thirst."

"They are, they are. Come in. Be careful."

"What a mess. A den. A lair."

"I sleep here. The bed's over there underneath all those newspapers and books. Upstairs, sometimes, I eat. Down here, mostly, I live."

"Whose paintings are these? Children's art."

"Mine. Thank you."

"I didn't know you were a painter too."

"Too? Neither did I. Do you want some whiskey? Some Scotch? Beer?"

"Maybe a little Scotch and water, please."

"Just Scotch. The water's too far away. Now sit down here ... here's a chair. Relax. Talk. Tell me what a bastard I am. How uncouth and everything."

"Oh, you're all right. Perfectly harmless. Just a little odd. Maybe a little paranoid as I told you before. Why do you teach?"

"Why do you?"

"Because I was trained to. Because I want to. I've always wanted to. Ever since high school when an English teacher told me I would make a good teacher someday. I never forgot that."

"That's how it all begins, this teaching business. It's always another teacher who passes it on. Why is that? Why do you think I'm such a bad teacher?"

"I don't know that you are a bad teacher. You're just not the kind of teacher most people expect. Not the type most parents would care to trust their son or daughter with."

"Never end a sentence with a preposition. You're trustworthy, huh?"

"Yes, I think so. This sounds terribly egotistical, but I am a model teacher. What parents and childen, even administrators expect a teacher to be, to represent."

"That's terrible."

"Hassock, you hate me."

"Try 'pity.' Are they dusting off the shelf for you, Elsie?"

"What do you mean?"

"I'm talking about Josie Sluer and the rest of her crew who I haven't even met, but I know they exist and are part of every goddam school in America. You know, those perfectly lovely gray-haired women who teach Longfellow and Chaucer, Hawthorne and Shakespeare. The people who spend most of their teaching lives reteaching grammar that, for some reason, was never quite taught properly the year before, when so-and-so was teaching it. Teachers whose whole life is gossip concerning students and other teachers. Those fragile bird-like bitches who think teaching means keeping a nice bulletin board with perfectly quaint pictures of New England and Stratford-on-Avon. Those wrinkled brains who think poetry is memorizing words and literature is a particularly good human being in the right historical time. You know who I mean, Elsie! Those women, and men, who administer death every day. All over America classrooms are filled with their deadly force. All over America poetry dies a little more each day in their dry, Listerened mouths. And Elsie, eventually they retire with a proper fanfare from the proper people — including proper students they succeeded in suffocating. And when they retire, Elsie, it's people like you who are waiting in line to fill their places. You've got all the qualifications. How old now, 32? 35? and never seriously been fucked? Not that it's going to make you a better teacher or anything. But it could be a beginning. Are you ready, Elsie? Ready to see where the American adventure really begins? Or will you be satisfied to spend summer after summer in search of tombstones? Here lies Sara Teasdale ... Elinor Wylie ... Sarah Kemble Knight ... Emily Dickinson ... 'My Life Closed Twice,' you know ... "

"You bastard!"

"Show me what's so sacred about teachers of literature and speech, sweetheart. Come to bed. Speech! We talk too much, Elsie. All of us. Come on, show me what you're saving for that life membership in the National Education Association."

"Hassock, get away from me."

"I've always wondered what it would be like to screw an old maid school teacher."

"Well, you're not going to find out, unless you rape this one."

"Would you like that, Elsie? Is that what it would take?"

"Auuuuuggggh . . ."

"What's that? Keep your hands off of me!"

"That's life upstairs, Elsie. Come on, give me your hand. I'll show you. Have no fear. I will not violate the vestal virgin."

"You're hurting me."

"Come, come. Up, up the backstairs. Move, move! Watch out for the thirsty plants. I've got to water those motherfuckers someday. Hurry, hurry. In here. Come in. see, see that worn human being on the bed. Old man, look! A vision! The Virgin Mary. Alive and in your room. Look at that . . . he's smiling!"

"You crazy bastard, let me go!"

"RUN, RUN, GO AHEAD! RUN HOME TO MOTHER. TAKE CARE OF HER TILL SHE DIES. WE'VE GOT SOMETHING IN COMMON. BOTH GOOD CHILDREN OF GOD. WE BOTH HONOR OUR FATHER AND MOTHER. BYE-BYE! wave, old man. Wave good-bye to the Virgin Mary, the Immaculate Conception, the Holy Lady who's never felt a man between her legs. Oh, old man . . . off to sleep, eh? Me too, I go down now, Me go down, clear off bed, maybe read a while, maybe be like Crakow. Maybe paint. Maybe write notebook. Sleep, Papa.

> Improvisation . . . the only way to teach . . .
> . . . to inspire to excess . . .
> a respect for things human . . .
> 9 dead Indians . . . The young are the old indeed . . .
> The young?
> I am the young!

"Clay! Clay! I've got a hot tape recorder for you from the audio-visual aids. Some dumb fuck left it outside the main circle, so I took it home over the weekend. Listen to the tape I made for you, for your class of darkies. A great black preacher from the Southside, the Reverend J.J. Jefferson. Man, wait till you hear his voice, the music, those people screaming and singing out of their skins! Talk to them about it. This is literature, man. This is it!"

"Thanks, Hassock. I'll give it a try."

"Where's everybody today? Elsie? Green-eyes?"

"Elsie says her doctor won't let her drink coffee anymore. Something

154

happen between you and her?"

"I don't remember. She's hopeless, Clay. Hopeless."

"You look like hell."

"No sleep. Too many nights... too long. Sometimes I think I could live my life from bed. I do need sleep. What the hell is this, almost winter already? Hurry summer. I need a vacation. Maybe go away for a while. Need a nurse to take care of the old man. No money for that. Shit."

"No money for what, Hassock?"

"Ah, Green-eyes. I feared you too abandoned me on this morning of sorrow and no sleep. Summer vacation. I'm dreaming summer vacation already just like a kid. But no money . . . nowhere to go."

"My aunt has a place up North," says Green-eyes. "Way up in Wisconsin. She's been trying to sell it for years, but never will. It's too far away for most Chicagoans who want a weekend summer place. I can have it all summer, anytime. You're free to use it, Hassock. Take your father along. I get up there sometimes in late August. Sometimes for a long weekend in fall."

"Wisconsin? Fuck Wisconsin. That's for the Indians. I'm a man of the world. I have visions of Greece, the Middle-East, the exotic. I hate Wisconsin. As a kid, that's the only place anybody from Chicago ever went. At least in my neighborhood. It was every factory worker's nirvana. 'I've rented a cottage on the lake in Wisconsin this summer, bla, bla, bla' 'We're taking the family to see the Indians at the Dells.' Turquoise rings, copper bracelets, totem poles, tomahawks and little birch bark canoes. All that commercial claptrap. Man, I've been to Sarajevo! Wisconsin holds nothing for me."

"Have you ever been there?"

"No."

"Typical Hassock."

"Okay... okay. Maybe I'll go. Get me a key. And I'll take the old man, if I have to. Did you ever see the word pictures of the Delaware Indians? All about creation? They're in *Adventures in American Literature.* Does anybody ever teach that Indian stuff I wonder?"

"Not that I know of," says Clay.

"I doubt it," says Green-eyes. "Just pictures. They really had no literature that I know of."

"No . . . no history either. Did anybody ever teach you about the Indians in high school? Me neither. I had one great history teacher though, Moss. He never got around to saying much about the Indians either except to mention that we gave them the royal screw. But nobody else even taught that!"

155

"Bell time," says Clay. "I'm gonna get me a headstart to class since Hassock over here has weighed me down with this damn tape recorder."

"Don't forget the P.T.A. tonight, you guys," says Green-eyes. "It's Open House, remember? Let's meet for a drink afterwards."

"What's Open House?"

"Hassock, if you'd empty that damn box of yours sometime, you'd know what the hell was going on around here," she smiles.

"Crakow takes care of it for me. Once a week he collects all the shit and burns it."

"Hassock, you're hopeless. Open House means that the parents come tonight and go through their kid's entire schedule, meeting the teachers. The periods are cut to only 10 minutes. All you have to do is explain the course, answer their questions, and smile. Smile, Hassock."

"Jesus."

"Happens only once a year," says Clay. A piece of cake for me. No parents ever show up for the Disadvantaged. So I just sit at the desk till it's all over."

"Good for you, Clay. But what about me?"

"You'll have a full house," Hassock, says Green-eyes. "With the caliber of kids you have, parents, aunts and uncles, grandmothers, plus all the kids will be there to show you off."

"I can't do it. There's more important things for me to do. Plus miles to go before I sleep."

"There's the bell. Have fun, Hassock," she says. "Listen, stick around this afternoon till my last class. We'll go to H.J.'s for supper, then I'll drive you home."

"Okay. I'll hide somewhere. What the hell am I going to do with all the parents? I'm not ready for them. Help!"

"See you, Hassock."

Bye-bye. So long. Goodbye. And there goes Hassock again fighting his way through the crowded hall in search of room #127. "Ouch, you're stepping on my feet." "Hey, who's grabbing me?" she smiles. Only me, Hassock, trying to make his way . . . ah, youth. Then a hand on his arm, "Are you the new man? The lock to my desk is broken in room #132. Can you fix it?" Hassock nodding no to her middle-age problems, then losing the back of her in another shuffle, now cresting toward her ass by inches, Hassock grinning and pinching a mean stretch of her girdled cheek. "Who did that? Did you touch me, young man?" Some innocent kid too young for the truth of such games. Go, go, Huck Hassock . . . get that damn raft downriver already . . . river stay away from my door . . . oh door, oh shit! Reckelson on shore.

"Hassock!"

"Get away from my door, or I'll huff and I'll puff and I'll blow you away."

"Not so fast. Serious problem . . . corporeal punishment. It's against the law in this state. What the hell are you trying to do? What's the story, Hassock? Why did you hit the kid?"

"Who told the version you heard?"

"It's all on this note. The notes I keep getting about your behavior in class."

"No name?"

"No."

"Let me see the handwriting."

"No."

"Then it's all a big lie. Don't believe everything you find in your box, Reckelson. I've never understood mystery anyway. You can't believe kids, you know that. Kids are all storytellers. They live in a fantasy world."

"Hassock, if I hear from Scutters on this, you're out. The end."

"Nope. Not yet."

"And you be here for Open House tonight. Wear some decent clothes. Shave. Get a haircut. Don't slam the door in my face! HASSOCK, I'M NOT THROUGH WITH YOU!"

"Everybody in? Good. Marvin, help me lock this door. There's a big wolf outside. Good, good. Go away, shoo, get out of here. Pull the shade down alongside the door. Thank You. Okay. Let's begin. Where were we? What's up for today, Jack?"

"Nothing. Same as usual."

"Correct. Good boy, Jack. You finally gave Hassock a correct answer. Well, just practice doing nothing for a few minutes while Hassock sorts out the day. I'm tired and hungry and on top of everything else, I'm faced with opening night at the old schoolhouse. Just leave me along for a bit."

The Green-eyed Nympho and a cup of coffee . . . "Her tongue was still busy in his mouth and this made it impractical to warn her of his impending fulfillment."

And there goes Horny Hassock checking the girls in class once again. Perfectly moral setup. They're studying and he's studying. Studying short skirts, legs, the infinite possibilities of desire. Emma? Not bad, though she does not yet understand her own legs. There's more to legs

157

than stretching. You must learn how to use those legs, Emma. Gloria, mmmm. Better. Almost womanhood. Diane . . . tilt! What hope for her? How can Hassock make your life more bearable? What to do for all the Diane Gurbals in all the high schools across America? What of the too thin? too fat? too ugly? The girls who will never be asked to any proms? I feel for all the Diane Gurbals, and all their hellish high school days. All the meanness made of them. All the humor. All the silence behind backs. Who can bear all that fat? You have Hassock's heart . . . but no desire. Hassock could not raise an erection for you if you performed the whole Kuma Sutra solo. "Nancy gave his tongue a last little pull and also moved her hand for him . . . " That's the story, Diane. In the minds of too many men, that's more real than you. And Joy. Oh, Joy! You make poor Hassock ache. Give us a cheer, Joy! Show us that tight little beachball ass beneath that skirt jumping up and down to save old New Highland High. But it's only the fullback's territory, eh? And what's left for dear old Hassock? Kirstin? The kindly Kirstin who sits in her own light like blue Danish glass? Kirstin of the nicely fashioned legs, swing out, swing in, in the natural rhythm of the act of love. Hassock feels an impending fulfillment. Kirstin-the-Quiet now crossing her legs again. Did you see that! "Nancy felt him harden against her hips, and ran her hands inside his shorts. She was not disappointed." Don't stand, Hassock. Remain seated. This too shall pass.

"I'M LOOKING FOR THE POETRY IN YOU PEOPLE! Wake up! Show me. Show me where it is. Jack, some poetry from your notebook. Anything, anything at all."

"Nothing, Hassock. I just don't understand what you want us to do."

"Marvin! Read . . . "

"I'm afraid I don't have what you want either, Hassock."

"Karl? Just nod you head yes or no . . . Nick?"

"Last summer my grandmother died. The day of the funeral, when we buried her, we had to put some flower petals on the casket. My father began to cry. I never saw my father cry before. And then I began to cry. There seemed to be no end to all the tears within both me and my father. The death of my grandma was the most emotional experience of my life so far."

"That's good, Nick. That's poetry all right. Death is very poetic territory. It's as good a place to begin as any. But why death from you young people? What about life? What about love and desire? Emma? Gloria? Diane? Kirstin? Joy? Nothing? You all have nothing to say? To feel poetic about? Look at it this way. You want a one word poem? Close your eyes. Apple. How's that? Apple.

"Now erase apple from your mind, and try these: BLUE ... WIND ... NIGHT. Open your eyes. What do you feel about those words? What do you associate? Watch Hassock. Watch Hassock put a poem on the board. Hassock's been making poems in bed for days and nights and months now. And now he opens his magic box and out pops poetry!

"EVERYTHING IS POETRY! LOOK AROUND YOU. TRULY LOOK! WATCH HASSOCK MAKE A POEM FROM THE DAILY NEWSPAPER. NEWSPAPERS ARE FULL OF POETRY. ATTACH YOURSELVES TO WORDS, TO FEELINGS, TO LIFE. MAKE POEMS. LOOK ...

> A sunny garden
> now is growing
> on the second floor
> of a
>   Chicago barn
> which once housed
> the horses
> for fire wagons

"You want love? Let's see what I can make of this fashion ad ...
> Oriental girl
> Down to the sea
>   Dabbles in color
> Waterfall
>   windfall
>   beach or boat ...
> Across the mountains
>   Crinkle
>   Crinkle
>   Sundown
>   doves

"Or here ...
> But what will she wear?
>   Pounds of jewelry
> Night sounds
>   and wild apples
> Skimming her
>   valley of wine and warmth

"Erase the board, someone. There's not enough space in this god room for all my poetry. Do you know Gertrude, eh? Of course you

She's an *Adventures in American Literature* reject. Lost in your genera-
tion and mine. But try her. Read Gertrude Stein sometime. There will be
days when she can save you with a single word . . .

TOTEM
FOR
G E R T R U D E
mad money
tokens
spare buttons
needle and thread
candies
perfume
earrings
rings
rain hat
saccharin
snuff
safety pins
paper clips
tea bags
instant coffee
cuff links
thumb tacks
nails
mailbox key
birdseed
and
even
pills

"This is for you guys:

STARTING   today,
children throughout the City
Poke GIANTS in the eye,
Hunt L E G E N D
shrink people
PLAY   K I N G in glass houses
Operate A
HAPPY
ENDING
Ole

"Enough? Or should we have some poems of pure joy?"

"Hassock?"

"Yeah, Marvin."

"I like that."

"Good. Me too, because they're mine. Because I made them. You will never understand that until you make *your* own — poems, paintings, books, whatever. Don't live secondhandedly! The poetry of other people is good for only a beginning. But it's nothing compared to the poems you hold inside yourself. Never rely on the imagination of others to live your life. You got the fire! Jesus, sometimes I think I could write a poem about *anything*. This greenhouse of a room. That powder blue fireplug outside the window . . ."

"What's a fireplug?"

"A FIREPLUG? How the hell did you people grow up? Haven't you ever played leapfrog over a fireplug? Haven't you ever opened them in the heat of summer? Do you know the city of Chicago at all, or is that forbidden teritory for suburban youth? Gloria?"

"Once a year my parents take me to the Art Institute and the Museum of Science and Industry."

"Jack?"

"We go downtown shopping a few times a month. Mainly to Field's and Carson's."

"And you've never been to Chinatown? Or Greektown? Germantown? Little Italy? Do you know that many of the Slav's are all close by on the Westside? And you've never tasted the food of these people? What the hell do you eat? How do you live? Where are the alleys in these suburbs? Or the sidewalks? Where are the children? The games? Is there any danger at all? The dim possibility of breaking a law and coming alive? I'm assigning, for homework this weekend, a trip to Sandburg's city of the Big Shoulders. All of you. Go! You must leave your parents home. You must travel there alone by El or train or bus. You must read some Sandburg along the way. Study some Nelson Algren during the next week. And some time, before the end of the year, read Richard Wright's *Native Son*, for a knowledge of the black life in Chicago. And keep those notebooks open through all this. Tell me what you feel and see. And write a poem about a fireplug!"

"What's a fireplug?"

"That short little character out there dressed in a powder blue with two stubby arms and a mushroom cap."

"Oh! You mean a fire hydrant!"

"Hmmm. You even got your own language around here, huh"

161

"Are you coming for Open House tonight, Hassock? My parents are coming." "Yeah, mine too." "Mine said they sure can't wait to see what this Mr. Hassock is all about."

"Out! OUT! Goodbye. Get lost. What is it, Kirstin? Ah, Kirstin, of course, of course. Thank you. You made my day."

"Crakow, this is really a great deal you've got down here. Thanks for letting me use the cot."

"Just stay. No hurry. I make more soup. Crakow stay late tonight too. Open House."

"Did your new man come yet?"

"I neber know. Maybe he come work night crew. Dunno. Crakow need vacation."

"We all do, Crakow. We all do. Listen, stop by my room when you get a chance, #127. I want another bolt or something on the inside of that door. Too many people always bothering. You got one of those latches that just slide into the doorframe?"

"No voory. Crakow fix."

"What's the season, old man? What's the hour?"

"Six-thirty."

"Six-thirty! Jesus, I was supposed to meet Green-eyes right after school!"

"Who?"

"A friend, just a helper. Where did you say the washroom was, Crakow?"

"Is broke here. Upstairs, upstairs in main circle. Go up, turn left, turn right, then in some more, then left, then right again. Big vooden door."

"How much time have I got?"

"Starts, 7. Is first class. Over, 8, 8:15."

"Got to go."

"Soup? Good tripe soup?"

"Next time, Crakow. Next time."

Up up up goes Hassock. See Hassock run! See Hassock turn! Round nd round the circle he goes. Gotta move, gotta hurry. Washroom, wash- om . . . where's the shithouse? Left . . . Right . . . In! Hassock here! Big den door, enter.

little man . . . a tiny man from a folk fable . . . an elf? a troll? . . . a troll cue-ball head. He sits upon the potty chair and his feet barely he floor.

"Are you the new man?" he asks. "Close the door, please, when you talk to me."

"Yes."

"A life saver! I'm out of paper. Will you run and get me some paper? I have to be in the circle any minute to welcome the parents. Do you know where they keep the paper?"

"No."

"Well ask Mr. Crakow. He's downstairs. Tell him that Principal Scutters needs some sanitary paper. Hurry, please. And take that flag down already. The sun has set."

Run, Hassock, run! Round and round and round and out and round once more and . . . FREE! Down ray #1, enter lounge . . .

"CLAY? CLAY!"

"Here, Hassock."

"Hey, you got the shirt on! Looks good. Listen, where the hell's that tape recorder?"

"In my car."

"Did you play it, Clay? What did they think?"

"Just loved it, Hassock. Some of 'em even started singing."

"Ha! Where do they get it, Clay? All that spirit? How do they keep it?"

"Beats me."

"More of the same, Clay. Teach them black. Understand? Stay with it. Here . . . here's a poem for them. Tell 'em Hassock wrote it. Put it on the board. Tell 'em 'nigger' is just a word they'll have to live with — just like Bohunk, Polak, Wop. We name ourselves in the end. We always do. That's the American way. Put this upon the board in big writing:

In NIGGER-TOWN the other day
    I saw a black iceman
Taking stairs two-at-a-time, two-at-a-time
    with a hunk of solid crystal in tow
        held by hungry tongs.
They swung all together
    in cool arcs
        then melted
in a varnished hallway of brass mailboxes
    and broken bells.

"You bring some of them to my class sometime. I doubt if my kids have ever met a black boy or girl. You bring them, and we'll talk and sing."

"You know, Hassock. I been thinkin'. You think I could teach them the whale? Maybe I'll move into *Moby* next."

"Do that, goddam it! Tell them the whale's black. You've lived with that whale all your fucking life. Go tell them about the whale, Clay. What it can do to a man. And listen, one last favor, please. Look at me, I'm a fucking mess. My shirt stinks, I need a shave. I can't go into that classroom in the shape I'm in. Hassock has to pull his old disappearing act with those parents. It's the end if I go in there. I want you to set that tape recorder up in my room. Put the tape of the Reverend J.J. Jefferson on, and wait till everyone's in there. Explain to them how I took suddenly ill, that you're the new man or something, and Hassock sends his greetings. He has a message for them. Then just turn that fucking tape on real loud and leave. I'll be hiding out in the parking lot. Tell Green-eyes to meet me there. And open the window. I want to hear J.J. Jefferson all the way in the parking lot."

Hassock absconding . . . a hand hooking him in the shoulder.

"Hey, man, where'd you get that shirt? You Hassock? I been hearing about you. That fucking lunchbox is too much, Dad!"

"Who the hell are you?"

"Arroyo. Arroyo L., old man. Art. The only fucking painter in the whole department. Everybody else is teaching art history or ceramic ash trays."

"I get the picture. So tell me, where the hell you been living while I been dying here?"

"Ray #8, man. Way out. The bitter end. Old Scutters doesn't even know it exists. He needs a passport to get out there. Ray #8 leads to Happy Hollow, where some of the kids smoke and fuck around after school. Near the dump. That's where they put Arroyo, right near the fucking dump! Hahahaha!"

"We have to talk sometime. I can't believe you exist. Right now I've got to make tracks. Look, the parents are coming down the halls already!"

"Follow me, Dad. Nobody'll find you in the Art Ray. Come on. I'll show you the kind of shit they give me to work with."

"What about you? Open House tonight?"

"Fuck it. I just set up a bunch of the kids' paintings and let the mommies and daddies ooo and ahhh them. I got nothing to say, man. I'm no talker. Visual, man. All visual."

"Arroyo, how come I never met you sooner? I might have survived all this."

"Hey, I got one of your chicks in class."

"Who?"

"Kirsten Wilkinson. Nice stuff."

164

"You sonofabitch! I didn't think there were two of us left in the whole goddam profession, let alone the same school. How the hell did they ever hire you?"

"Good old fashioned American politics. They had to. My uncle's on the school board."

"You know Scutters?"

"Never saw the cat."

"I don't think he exists myself."

"Here we are, old boy, the Art Department. Most of the good shit on the wall's mine. This is it, man. The whole Art Department: two fucking studios. Catch that door. Lock it. Shot a brandy? How about a nice long ceegar! Ah! Light up. Nobody'll bother us in here."

"You got a department chairman?"

"Yep. Goober."

"Goober?"

"Goober. He paints Dresden dolls and sells that in the art fairs."

"Jesus. How the fuck do they find these people, Arroyo? Don't they realize what it does to the kids?"

"I don't know, man. They sure do dig them up. I got an old twat here teaching ceramics who makes nothing but chartruse boomerang-shaped ash trays. She's a beaut. Hates my fucking guts. I keep sneaking in there and reshaping her clay in the best male and female anatomy I can design."

"Arroyo, I can't believe you're here."

"Believe it. Stick around, friend. There's more. Hey, you want to paint?"

"I'd love to. An untrained eye, though."

"Good. That's what I'm looking for. Too many of these damn kids spent too many years in grade school cutting out orange pumpkins and red hearts."

"Same thing in English. They think poetry begins and ends with 'Hiawatha'."

"If you see anything of mine you like, take it."

"No shit?"

"It yours."

"Even this soft blue nude here, holding the balloons? Jesus, it's beautiful."

"Sold. I can't hang it in the halls. Too obscene. Such shit."

"Thank you, buddy. I'll love her forever."

"Catch this new piece of sculpture I'm working on over here. I've got all these crankshafts from the dump back there. The way it's going to work is like this: You turn it by hand, you see, and instead of pistons I'm making these big pink tits with red nipples that will come flying out at you, Bam! Bam! Bam! A tit twittering machine."

"Exhibit it in my room when you're finished."

"A deal."

"In fact, I'd like you to come by sometime soon and just talk about art. Or do it, or something."

"Sure. Lots of stuff we can do."

"Work in the writing?"

"Hell yes. Talking pictures or something!"

"Perfect. Room #127. Knock three times."

"Hey, I got something else you might be interested in. A merry-go-round."

"A real one?"

"What's real, man? You know, these kids don't even know what the hell a street carnival is! As soon as I get enough bread, or can latch onto enough supplies, I'm going to build a whole fucking carnival, all out of wood and canvas. I've got plenty of motors to run the stuff. A Ferris wheel, side shows, booths of kewpie dolls, the whole fucking show, man."

"A noble endeavor, Arroyo. Count me in. We'll set it up late some night in the main circle. If they throw us out, we'll move it to Happy Hollow or the dump. You be the merry-go-round man, I'll be a barker or a clown."

"Hey, can you see it, man! Can you see it! Why the hell aren't you teaching art?"

"I can't even teach English."

"You want to see the merry-go-round?"

"Hell yes."

"Drink up. It's in the boiler room. By Crakow. Don't forget the painting. Here, let me get your lunch box."

"So you know Crakow too?"

"Yeah, a horny sonofabitch. Sometimes I go down there to work late with a nude model. I rap the pipes three times to let Crakow know what's happening. He's out there in the dark, peeking behind the furnace, taking it all in. A good guy, though. Makes great soup. Besides, he keeps the beer cold. Come on."

"Do we have to go through that main circle again? I don't understand it."

"The only way, man. Stick with me, I'll guide you through. Nobody'll spot you in that shirt anyway. You look like a fucking janitor. Okay, let's run!"

"I tell you, I get lost in this goddam circle. Hey, wait. You say you never saw Scutters?"

"No man. And I don't give a shit."

"Open that door over there. Just an inch."

"This one?"

"Yeah."

"Are you that new man? Where's the paper?"

"Holy shit!"

"That's your man. In the flesh."

"Here's the red doorknob, let's head down. Crakow, you old fuck, where are you?"

"Ah, crazy man. Hey, Hassock, you too? You know this bozo? Some beer, huh?"

"You got it, old man. Comes payday, I'll buy you a case. I owe you. Crakow, how'd you like that piece of ass I had down here the other afternoon?"

"Vhat?"

"Vhat? You know vhat!"

"Oh, you mean vone with the mellons like this?"

"Heah, yeah."

"Vas nice woman."

"You bet your ass."

"Not my ass. Voman's ass! Hahaha."

"Think you can handle something like that, Crakow?"

"Oh, Crakow go up like this arm, see! Umph!"

"You horny old bastard you. Listen, put the lights on for us over there. I want to show Hassock the merry-go-round."

"Sure, sure, you just go."

"Follow me, Hassock. This way. Look, over there. See it?"

"Goddam. Beautiful, Arroyo, beautiful. Even a red and white canope, eh?"

"Yeah. That chick, Kirstin, made that. Only four riders — all friends of mine, men, women, kids. Two more riders to go. How about you and me, huh? Shit, man, I could draw your face anytime. You look like Zapata with that mustache. You want to see it work? Get on. No music yet. Get on, Hassock. It'll hold the both of us."

"I like it . . . there's something sad about the way it turns, but I sure do like the feel of it all . . . "

"They'll be music . . . calliope music . . . and colored lights."

"Why are you wasting your time at Highland High? You should be in New York, Europe, the West. You've got too much imagination for this

167

place. They'll kill you in the end, you know that."

"Don't worry, Dad. Once I have the bread, goodbye High-High. Here, have another ceegar."

"The hell with the bread. Go. Nobody's going to give a damn about you here. But the kids . . . yeah, the kids."

"Think so? Yeah. But it takes bread to make a move, man. And as soon as I get it, it's gone. I'll never get out of here."

"You've got to. You just get your ass out of here by the end of the year. Read some Henry Miller. Do you read?"

"I hate words."

"Well, goddam it, read Miller. I'll bring you some Miller to read. He's a painter too. *The Angel is My Watermark.* I'll start you with *The Tropics.* He'll show you why you've got to get the fuck out of here."

"Hassock, you know who the Balloon Girl is on the painting?"

"No. But she resembles . . . "

"Kirstin. She's some young lady."

"Arroyo, tomorrow there's going to be a new flannel shirt for you in my lunchbox. And a copy of Henry Miller's *To Paint is to Love Again.* My only copy. I don't need it anymore. My whole head's a watercolor these days."

"Yeah. I like to see things that way."

"Make yourself at home, Green-eyes. Come on to bed. A good day, eh? One of my best. Don't even tell me what happened at the Open House. I'd rather imagine it."

"Clay will never be the same. He stood in the dark outside and watched it all. And when the parents started to leave, he began throwing stones at the window. I don't know how many he broke, how many people he may have hit."

"Good man Clay. He' going to teach that fucking whale, did I tell you?"

"Are they ready for it?"

"Shit, they're ready for anything if they have the right teacher. You want to make some coffee on the back stove? And check on the old man again? He was almost asleep when we came. You're going to stay the night with me, okay? You know, here I am a grown man, and I'm still afraid of the dark. I don't understand myself. As a kid, I had so much fear. And for a long time I was afraid I'd crack up. That still haunts me. I don't know if I'm there again or past that stage. The last few nights have been hell down here in the basement. I see the old man coming for me. I see the old lady over there at the tubs washing clothes. Once I saw her in the backyard watering the flowers at night. I painted this poem for her beside the bed:

Around the GARDEN
Red Giants
       and White Dwarfs
          Attempt to assassinate BLACK-EYED SUSANS
       TOMATOES
          bounce off
             the ground floor
       Grass   S P A R K S
       Wildflowers Whistle
                W H I T E

"I'll get the coffee, Hassock. Keep talking. I can hear you."

"Move in with me, Green-eyes. There's room. We can live upstairs if you like. We can make this into a kind of studio. You've got to really meet Arroyo sometime. See if he reminds you of me. It's crazy. We're like family. He's building his own merry-go-round, did I tell you? Down in Crakow's boiler room. I rode it. It's all white. All made of wood and canvas. He's painted the faces. And I'm going to be one of the riders. Imagine that! Clay's got to meet him. I can't understand why all you guys haven't met. Too departmentalized a school, I guess. Imagine giving me a beautiful painting like this, and I only just met the guy? Let's hang it over there at the foot of the bed. That'll be good for both sleeping and waking."

"He's sound asleep."

"He's still alive? I was afraid when I went in there before that he might be dead. I was gone all day and night."

"You can't leave him alone that long again."

"No, no."

"I read, write, paint. Clip newspapers. Sometimes I ride the El down to Chicago and get drunk with some writer friends — O'Roaragan, Loneson, whoever's around. Brave men. A different breed. They have a piece of it all. But not as big a piece as the painters like Arroyo. The writers are all head. But the painters are all eyes. There's more silence to them. And that may be more important."

"You think you'll have a job tomorrow?"

"My days are numbered. I won't make it through spring, I know."

"Fight them, Hassock. I'll help you."

"It doesn't matter. But I'm not through with those fucking kids yet. Say, where's my lunchbox? Hand it here, will you. That kid, Kirstin. She gave me some work today from her notebook. The only one who wrote any poems . . .

169

Are
we
a   Let's
poem?   sink
                                     roses
                                     in
                                     the
                                     snow.

          Stoplights
                are
                     Revolutionary
                          Green
                               targets.

"My god, I think I've got me a poet, Green-eyes . . .
                              The day
                                   I came back
                                        from before,
                                   The weeds were
                                        beginning again.

     Come April, Hassock,
          I will scoop the hour
               and hurl midnight snow to stars.
     In worm warm earth,
          I'll plant a field of birds for you
               to split the sun.

"Green-eyes! A poet! Only eight dead Indians!"
"That last one is beautiful, Hassock. I think she's in love with you."
"Come to bed, Green-eyes. Come to sleep. Time passes, eh? What's
the season? Winter? Spring? Take that watercolor down over there,
would you please? For Kirstin tomorrow. Leave it near my lunchbox. Do
you think she'll like it? Two suns — orange and Prussian blue. Crazy
watercolors of mine. I can't imagine where they all come from. Not as
good as the Balloon Lady. But good enough. They are mine."
"Why all the suns?"
"I don't know. I don't know. They just come out that way. Maybe because inside, it's very dark. Come to bed, Green-eyes. You'll live with me,
eh? For a while?"
"For a while."

"Good, good. Hassock is so tired, but he still wants to make love. Do your stuff, Green-eyes. Keep me alive. Hassock hates to sleep. Hates to close his eyes. So, have you been reading Saroyan?"

"Mmmmmm."

"Good, good. He's a good place to begin. You should read his stuff to your kids. Fuck all those reading machines. I must tell my own kids about Saroyan sometime soon. There is one of his stories in *Adventures in American Literature,* you know. Not one of his best, but still Saroyan. With Saroyan how can there be good and bad? An Indian story no less. 'Locomotive 38, the Ojibway.' They won't understand it, I know. I've tried to teach it once before. They never understand it. They don't like it. I didn't like it either the first time I read it. The Indian has all the answers, you see. He doesn't do a goddam thing, hardly says a word, but he has all the answers, all the life. They won't understand that. Ah, how I wish we had Saroyan's 'The Time of Your Life' in the book. That would be something. Do you know it? Oh, Green-eyes, I'm so glad to feel you next to me. 'The Time of Your Life,' now that would be an adventure for them! They could use those opening words . . . which I've forgotten . . . how did they go? . . . 'In the time of your life, live — so that in that good time there shall be no ugliness or death for yourself . . .' I can't remember the rest. There is something, though, something near the end of that passage that I've never understood. I wish Saroyan would explain it to me . . . 'If the time comes in the time of your life to kill, kill and have no regrets.' What do you think he means, Green-eyes? Don't tell me. Turn off the light. Hold me. I'm afraid."

"You see, the story has no end. Put that down in your notebooks if it matters to you. Better yet, put your own stories in those notebooks. And remember, I want to see those notebooks sometime. I want to see what kind of stories you people can tell. And if they are very good stories, the beginning, the middle, the end do not matter. Only the life that was there and is now part of you. We write, always, our own lives you see. That is the story."

"Hassock?"

"Yes?"

"There's someone at the door."

"Ignore them."

"He's got his own key."

"Crakow!"

"Hullo, Hassock. I suppose to fix vindows. Some bozo break three vindows last night Open House. I fix door too."

171

"Okay, Crakow. Hey, wait. Something's very funny here. What's so funny, class? Oh, I see. Crakow, Crakow's the funny man! The DP. The greenhorn. The unsuburban American. It's funny how he talks, huh? He really breaks you up. Crakow, excuse these poor ignorant bastards. Come here. I want you to meet my dead Indians."

"Hullo. I go fix vindows, Hassock. No mind. Teach."

"Fuck the windows, Crakow. Sit, sit. Show these people your hands. They never really saw the likes of you before. Tell them about yourself."

"Agh, they vould not be interested."

"Tell us about the old country, where you came from, stuff like that."

"Live in village called Prock on Vista River. Father was all the time stone mason. Vas nice there, but vas hard. Here, is good life. Vork. Money. I save, me my wife, Zdenka, have two-flat, income property. One son go college, become businessman. I help. I help."

"Question . . . Gloria."

"Where do you live?"

"In city. Blue Island. Know Blue Island?"

"What do you do for fun?"

"Fun? Play cards. Lots of pinochle. Eat. Dances, the lodge hall. Picnics, summer, in forest preserve. Drink beer. Vhat you mean?"

"Kirstin, over there, has a question, Crakow."

"Are you happy?"

"Sometimes, agh, mostly time is happy. When I drink the beer . . . very happy, eh Hassock?"

"What makes you unhappy, Crakow?" asks Hassock. "Do you know any stories?"

"Unhappy, huh . . . stories . . . Vell, old. Getting old. Not like you, all young. Get to be old man, old voman. Is sad. Is story. In village vas young man name . . . Sadko. In love with baker's daughter, next village. But baker make daughter marry rich farmer, and Sadko, nother time, some years, marry other voman, plain voman his village. They live a long time. Leave village. Come to America. Have family. Make much money. Get old. Happy? Agh, maybe. But all the time, Sadko old man, still love baker's daughter. And in here, in head, still sees her. And baker's daughter always young."

"Hassock, or Mr. Crakow?"

"Yeah, Jack."

"That story doesn't make much sense."

"Up your ass, Jack. You really piss me off. You heard the man, didn't you? He was telling what he remembered. That's all anyone can do. You were lucky enough to be in his presence, his world. What the hell can you share? Crakow, thank you. It was fine. Forget the windows for now. We all thank you for coming to class."

"Goodbye, Mr. Crakow." "Thank you, Mr. Crakow." "Bye."

"Form a circle around the desk. I want to read to to you. Happiness, huh? Crakow. That reminds me of a poem by Carl Sandburg . . .

> I asked professors who teach the meaning of life to tell me what is happiness.
> And I went to famous executives who boss the work of thousands of men.
> They all shook their heads and gave me a smile as though I was trying to fool with them.
> And then one Sunday afternoon I wandered out along the Desplaines river
> And I saw a crowd of Hungarians under the trees with their women and children and a keg of beer and an accordian.

"So there. Now for another adventure in American literature. You know, the strange thing about this kind of story I have in my hand is something I have only recently discovered. Talk about beginnings and endings! This has neither. You open the book anywhere, like a Bible, and begin to read. Poetry is like that. And people. Maybe that's the way books are meant to be made. Any book that demands any imagination at all.

"Here, listen to Hassock. Feel these words. Notice how they work yet say so little . . . 'Both were now worked up to a fever pitch and neither wanted further delay. Armond broke their embrace and Nancy sank to the couch. She quickly swung her legs up on it and then lay back and separated them. She raised her knees in the age-old invitation and held out her arms to him, but she realized that this desire was wholly physical, without the emotional involvement she had experienced with Jim. Then he was on his knees between her thighs and further thought was submerged in a wave of purely physical feeling. She reached between their bodies but before her hand found him, he found her body with his and entered. The motion was sudden but Nancy was prepared for it and found it intensely pleasant. Armond started his motion at a pace that indicated that he planned to run a short race and this suited Nancy's own desires. Her lips found his and again their tongues met. Nancy felt her peak approaching and wondered if they would reach the end together.'

"See? What do you feel? SIT STILL! DON'T WALK OUT ON ME.

NOT FINISHED! COME BACK! DON'T GO! STAY!"

"Hassock, that's the bell."

"Don't go yet."

"But we'll be late."

"Goodbye. Goodbye. Kirstin, wait. I have your poems in my lunch-box. I have a gift for you, wait. Come, take me to the Happy Hollow. Your hand, your hand, please, in mine."

"What's the season, little woman? It seems a little cool for spring. Here, put on my shirt. The wind is strong, stay warm. The sun seems broken into a million pieces. Did you plant that field of birds for me to split the sun? Happy Hollow. A good name for such a place. Only the kids could have thought of that. A place to 'smoke and fuck around' Arroyo says. Come, little woman, lay down beside me. Let us smoke and open to ourselves. What a distraction you have been to me. What an attraction in class. What an inspiration, only a real teacher would know. Something like love, perhaps. Though others would bad-mouth it, calling it lust. Little women like you who can drive a teacher mad. There should be one of you in every class. A Hassock in every school. An Arroyo too. He gave me that painting of you with the balloons. I shall have you, in this way forever. Do you see the importance of these acts? All gifts. Ah, such thighs. I could write a magic marker poem on each one of them. And an X to mark what the Hopi called in their creation myth, *sipapuni,* Place of Emergence. What will become of those eight dead Indians, eh? What can we do for that dull boy, Jack? Help Hassock. And what about Marvin? Karl? Nick? Nick, perhaps, will come around. It's in his blood. And what of the girls, eh? That cheerleader with her fullback? Those two future clubwomen, Emma and Gloria? And the curse of Diane? Oh, I wish so many other worlds for them. To make them paint. To show them Tivoli. To preserve the child in man. Do you see what Arroyo is after? And still love, There is so much to teach by not teaching. I've hardly begun. I never even got to the Indians. Oh, there is so much there. Love me, little woman."

"Time passes, eh, old man? *Cinco de la tarde.* What's the season? And where are those fucking bulls? Never trust a son, old man. He goes out into the world, loses his head, forgets to come home, then leaves you to die alone. The house has gone to seed, old man. The yard's a fucking jungle, wild weeds and red poppies. I've never learned to live with grass. We never understood each other's time. Better a daughter, old man. Better a stay-at-home daughter than an incorrigible son. Women never

kill the way men do. Death to the name of the father, eh? We do ourselves in. Death, I'm beginning to live with. It may be life after all. Come
up, old man, down to the basement with me. Why there's nothing to you
at all.

"Green-eyes, look what I found. Should I sit him up or lay him out on
the bed? Green-eyes, are you here? Elsie, so you haunt me still? I am
nothing but a child you say? I want everyone to love and praise me? Yet I
run from real life? Agh. What do you know? Be still . . . running in circles
from the real . . . what kind of answers do you provide for the young? Fantasy. More fantasy. You can't make a life out of merry-go-rounds. People
only *visit* Tivoli. The gates open and close every day. Walk through your
Tivoli after the hour. Where is the music? Your colored lights? Your fireworks? Your love? You are not a teacher, Hassock. Only a clown. A blight.
You prey on the weak. Clay, over the edge again, just for the meaning of a
stupid whale! Loss of mind and livelihood — thanks to you. And Carol,
gone, missing. You drove her out of teaching, away from something to
hold onto. Good work, Hassock. Are you proud? Reckelson, concerned
enough to take a chance with you, was almost fired. You tried, oh how you
tried, to do the whole system in. But in the end, you failed. You under-
estimated the responsibility of the young today. They had a much better
hold of themselves than you, Hassock. Smart enough to lead you on all
the while. To accept superior marks without even listening to you. To
turn you in — one of them, at least. Though sooner or later, all of them,
I'm sure. The notes kept coming. Principal Scutters found out, you see.
The whole school was aware of the note from your student to the principal, describing your final antics in class, and your involvement with Kirstin Wilkinson in Happy Hollow that afternoon. She's been transferred
to a half-way house for her own good. Her diagnosis, mild schizophrenia,
brought on by drugs. Happy Hollow has been burned down to the ground
and bulldozed over, by the orders of the school board. Right triumphs
over all. Why didn't you try to teach them that? There's your answer . . .
Oh, Elsie, Elsie, I was never any good in handling such easy answers. I
sought the mysteries, the imponderables: life, love, truth, beauty, and
death. Truth triumphs after all. That's why Reckelson had to be inform-
ed of what was going on. And that's why, in the end, I had to tell Scutters,
too. My time was up. I knew it. My kids, all of them, are absolved. Some
day they may know the truth: Hassock had to do himself in. Let that be a
lesson for them. Let them know that it is necessary at times to kill without
regret. And love. Even the likes of you. Ah, Green-eyes, where are those

175

notebooks? I WANT A HAPPY ENDING, GODDAM IT! DEATH SITS THERE ON THAT FUCKING CHAIR AND STARES AT ME! NURSE, WHERE ARE THOSE GODDAM NOTEBOOKS? BRING ME MY MAIL! AND DON'T CALL ME 'TEACH'."

Dear Hassock,

You got me to start writing essays and poetry of my own because you gave me a new look at literature. I never did like to read much, but class discussion brought out things I had never thought about before. All our notebooks were collected by someone from Principal Scutter's office. I don't have anything to show you right now. But I'll send you something next time.

Sincerely,
Karl Hinds

Hi Hassock,

Well, we got Mr. Reckelson back again. And we're studying grammar like it was something he invented. God, I never knew before just how boring grammar can be. He says we're probably not going to study anymore literature for the rest of the year because we're so far behind. But when he found out we hadn't even gotten to Emerson or Thoreau, he said he'd have to make us read that on our own without discussion. My history teacher mentioned that guy, Zapata, you told us about. I went down to the Chicago Public Library and took out a bunch of books about him. He was really something, wasn't he? There are still a lot of people in that country who believe he never died. But my teacher says we aren't going to study him because that's Mexican history. Take care of yourself.

Sincerely,
Marvin

Hey Hassock,

I wrote a poem for you—

    I
    Hate
    School
            maybe not a very good poem, but like you said,
it's MY POEM! I can't think of anything else creative to
write because I'm in a shitty mood in this class, and this
class is Economics, and what it all adds up to me is
D U M B. Plus I'm surrounded by these ugly girls. And I
mean ugh ugly. I wouldn't even use one of these to bait my
fish hook. Someday I'd like to find one like the last story
you read us. Where can I get a copy of THE GREEN-
EYED NYMPHO? Or some of that guy Saroyan's stuff?
That DARING YOUNG MAN book? I have a feeling I'm
going to be called on . . . yep.
                        Bye,
                            Nick.

Dear Mr. Hassock,

    The question or idea called conformity bothers me. For
some reason, which I'm not sure of yet, I don't want to
follow everybody else, but I continue to do it. Somewhere
inside of me I think conformity is wrong for the individual
but good for society. I think it takes guts to be different, or
it takes something many people like myself just do not
have. In psychology, conformity is expressed as a need for
every teen. The teacher said people don't like to be different and will do things they don't really want to just to be the
same. I think this is true because on the first day of school
this year I wore cowboy boots. A few of my friends mocked
me so I changed back to the ordinary, common shoe. I think
now I may go back to the cowboy boot because I feel better
wearing them, and they are more comfortable. Does it
really matter what others say? I realize this is very minor,
and it doesn't take much guts to do this kind of thing, but it
is a beginning. I'll let you know what happens.

                        Good luck,
                            Jack Smith

Dear Hassock,

There are so many things I would like to voice my opinions about and many people. I would like people to listen to. But there is no one. You said if you write things down, you have your own captive audience. So since I do have the time and the energy, and no fear of getting a poor mark or severely criticized, I'll say what's on my mind.

First of all, I would like to tell you of this terrible fear I have of being alone. I know, realistically, there is a God, and in my belief, he will never leave me alone. Still, I get an awful feeling that one day I'm going to be left sitting in a modern house somewhere in suburbia, with the walls slightly in need of paint, dusty furniture, and a brand new organ with colored keys that any dummy can play. And I'll be sitting at that organ alone, asking myself, why? This picture comes to me sometime in a dream and frightens me more than anything. What causes such dreams, Hassock? In my case, I think I was forced to take responsibility too young, and even now, I feel I have too many things to carry on my shoulders. I'm not asking for pity. I just want to understand my fear. I think the loss of my father, and other things, may have much to do with me.

And I would like to say something about love. I suppose everyone else in class has had something to say on the subject, because you were always talking about it. But here it is from a different perspective. I have never shown this to anyone in my life. I have never really looked at it myself. Suppose a young girl has a mother who is an alcoholic? When she is sober, she gives the girl almost everything she wants. But when she is drunk, which is more frequently, she tells her she loves her but doesn't want her. I suppose by throwing out a question to you: 'Is that love?' doesn't solve anything. But it helps me see everything better by writing it all down.

I wonder if this is love? Sometimes I suspect it's all an act. And other times it feels very real.

I miss you, Hassock.

Love,
Emma Asbridge

178

Hassock,

You are truly a great man. I think you are. Yours was the only class I could enter and enjoy. It made the rest of the day bearable. I never knew what would happen next in our class. It was all a kind of surprise everyday. Maybe that's why it was so great. I used to read mysteries just for the plot. But you taught me to care about people in stories. Real people on the street too, which is hard to explain.

You taught me to love poetry and beauty and to lift my face toward the sun and the cloudless sky. You taught me to love a simple person and a crying child. You made me laugh, you made me cry ... like now . . .

Hassock, you and your crazy mustache!

Love,
Gloria

Mr. Hassock,

I never had very much to say in class. (I seldom speak up in any class.) And I don't think you liked me very much. (Most teachers don't.) But I just wanted you to know that I wish you were back. You remind me a lot of my Uncle Stash who comes over the house every Friday night to play cards with my father and friends. He usually ends up getting very drunk and telling these very funny stories. You'd like my Uncle Stash.

Sincerely,
Diane Gurbal

Hassock,

I'm insane. INSANE! I've got to be the strangest person I've ever had the experience of meeting. I'm forever contradicting myself. But only out of confusion. I really need people badly. I'm vulnerable to the slightest insult.

I HATE SEX FIENDS! I can't understand why God made the ten commandments if the only reason he put man and woman on earth in the first place was to populate this global paradise. It just doesn't make sense. I'm continually finding myself torn between my religious beliefs and my natural instincts. What's the answer, Hassock? One minute I feel a great yearning to let go of everything I've been taught, and just go screw! And the next minute I feel as if I were condemning myself to hell forever for even thinking such thoughts. And the next minute I feel restricted, tied up in knots of other people's morality, and I want to cut loose once again. I swear to God I'm insane. I want to laugh when I'm extremely upset and deeply hurt. I want to cry at the slightest indication of good, love, joy. But I don't do either one well.

I can't understand how a person can be so damn obsessed with the idea that life is sex. I know a boy who thinks that football, driving fast cars, drinking beer and screwing broads is all that matters. IT SICKENS ME SO MUCH I COULD PUKE!

Oh, I'm all confused. You should know what I really think when I'm all alone late at night. I tell you, Hassock, I'm INSANE!

Sincerely yours,
Joy

For Hassock,

Propositional Poem

1. Come
2. Unto
3. Me

Story

Then the little man with the white parachute jumped off the curb and boarded an oak vessel bound for Corner Hole in Fireplug Bay down the river Ever. He was detained, though, by a crinkly crinkly paper marked BUTTERFINGER and fractured twig that had visions of one day becoming a diving rod. So when the rains came (as rains always do in the end) and the wind (as it always does in the beginning) lifted everything free — including the man who ascended in the white parachute.

Words

I'm at the Riverbank Halfway Home only the river
is more like a sewage canal.
I got your address through Arroyo who got it from I
don't know where and spread it around to the rest
of the class. Including Mr. Clay's black kids. So
you may hear from them too.
Arroyo says hello and that he hates to write but
that he hopes to see you sometime. He's going
West. He's funny. He sneaks in here to visit me on
Saturday mornings. He wears a long black over-
coat, a funny hat, and carries an attache case. He
tells the lady at the front desk that he is Principal
Scutters and she lets him right in. His pockets are
filled with colored balloons.
My five-year-old brother brought me a bunch of
his paintings yesterday. I'm enclosing one for you.
Pretty, isn't it?
Whenever I looked at you, the most astounding
thing was your eyes — they always appeared to be
thoughtful, bright, observant, sad, and *so alive.*
After you told us about some of the things you see,
I realized that I really have no vision yet. Sometimes I had the urge to shrink so small that I could
climb inside your head to see what you see and
what you're all about.
    faded china cups and exploding cigars,
        blue balloons and magic boxes too . . .
    I guess everything is too much,

            Your little woman, K,
                in the Castle
                by the river

P.S. I'm sending you a book by Gibran.
Why did you do it?
What are you about, anyway?

"What am I about? Is that the question? Begin again."

And then what? And then what? How does it all end, Hassock?

"Some say he returned to his old neighborhood, disappeared, probably died."

And what do the others say?

"That he was bundled up in a blanket in the back seat of a red Ford and left somewhere in Wisconsin under a new moon, to watch the sun, stalk the Indian in him, and wait in silence for another fall."

Now when I get back
I expect to find all of you
running through the streets
holding great bunches of wildflowers
—Kenneth Patchen

Other Books by Norbert Blei . . .

The Watercolored Word (1969)

" . . . is a fantastic (no overstatement) have enter the world of poem . . ."
— *Small Press Review*

The Hour of the Sunshine Now (Story Press, 1978)

"Blei quietly experiments with the surreal, with poetry, myth, image . . . a man to watch."
— *Publisher's Weekly*

"A worthwhile addition to collections of modern fiction."
— *Library Journal*

"One of the best writers in the Midwest."
— Henry Kisor, Chicago *Sun-Times*

"He has all the equipment, skills, discipline, and scope of vision, plus an invaluable element, a fine, deep sense of humor."
— Don Skiles, *American Book Review*

The Second Novel (December Press, 1979)

"One hundred years from now *The Second Novel* will be in print regardless of what else Norbert Blei writes. . . . because it it a great book."
— Harold Grutzmacher, Door County *Advocate*

" . . . an intriguing revelation of the process as process, or artifice as artifice, often humerous, as directly relating the throes of writing can only be."
— *Library Journal*

Door Way (Ellis Press, 1981)

"A fascinating assemblage of profiles that adds up to a vivid, feeling portrait of a region."
—Studs Terkel

"I predict that, someday, his Door County will join the great mythical-real landscapes that include Salinas, Spoon River and Yoknapatawpha."
—Harry Mark Petrakis

"Blei has a fine ear and a genuine, searching, feeling humanity that is evident in dozens and dozens of observations."
—John D. Callaway, Chicago *Tribune*

"I honestly believe it is a small American classic, and if there were any justice it would be read — and taught — widely."
—Willard Manus

" ... a necessary option. Blei, who has been widely published, writes of Door County, Wisconsin in a way that brings it and the lives of its people vividly to the imagination. Not to be missed."
—*Library Journal*

Door Light (Ellis Press, 1983)